AFTER THE FALL

a life of *strength* through *weakness*

illustration by Jack Fischer

J. Fischer
2000

JACK FISCHER
with *Joyce Lister*

Note: The information in this book is for educational purposes only and is not recommended as a means of diagnosing or treating an illness. All matters concerning physical and mental health should be supervised by a health practitioner knowledgeable in treating that particular condition. Neither the publisher nor author directly or indirectly dispense medical advice or assume any responsibility for those who choose to treat themselves.

Published in Northridge, California, by Fischers Of Men Press. Fischers Of Men Press is an independent publishing venture created by author Jack Fischer.

Fischers Of Men Press

Jack Fischer can be contacted at: fischersofmenpress@gmail.com

Cover Layout and Design by Nadine Erickson.
Nadine can be reached at: oaxacasons@yahoo.com

Interior Layout and Design by Joshua Rubinstein.
Joshua can be reached at: josh@jdruby.com

ISBN 978-0-9986315-0-9

Fischer, Jack, 1955 –
    After The Fall : A Life of Strength Through Weakness / Jack Fischer
    1. Fischer, Jack, 1955 – 2. BIO018000 Biography and Autobiography, Religious,
    3. BIO026000 Biography and Autobiography, Personal Memoir, 4. SPO017000
    Sports and Recreation Gymnastics

ATF - 001pb

Printed in the United States of America by IngramSpark.
IngramSpark can be found at:
https://www.ingramspark.com

❧ Table of Contents ❧

Pride Goes before Destruction - page 1

Part 1: Early Challenges - page 7

Part 2: Flip Flops - page 17

Part 3: Strength in Weakness - page 37

My Grace is Sufficient for You - page 77

"I vividly remember the first time I met Jack Fischer. It was at a church where I was speaking, and I was immediately impressed with this young gymnast. Strong and athletically fit, it was clear he was heading for the Olympics. Then, just a few days later, a catastrophe occurred that changed his life forever.

Over the decades, I have watched this man's discipline and perseverance turn what was once a tragedy into a remarkable triumph of faith and endurance – and the lessons he has learned can help you become an over-comer, too.

Be inspired by Jack's remarkable story, and be assured that the same God who has sustained him, will sustain you, no matter how tragic your circumstances!"

– *Joni Eareckson Tada*

Joni and Friends International Disability Center

We all need heroes—ordinary people who do something extraordinary. Most often the heroes in the news or movies are those who rise up for a moment in time. How can we ever forget the heroism of the first responders on 9/11 who rushed into collapsing buildings in order to save others? Or Todd Beamer and his fellow passengers sacrificing themselves to take down Flight 93 in order to save our White House? These are inspiring, but they are only one example of heroism.

Christopher Reeve, the man who played the hero of heroes, Superman, would offer us another example. A hero is an ordinary individual who finds the strength to persevere and endure in spite of overwhelming obstacles.

These heroes may never make the news because their stories take too long to tell, but we all rub shoulders with unsung heroes who have amazing stories of overcoming incredible obstacles in everyday life. Jack Fischer is one and his story is inspiring.

I never knew Super-Jack, the Olympic level gymnast. If I had met him, I'm not sure we would have anything in common. I never even made the football team and here is a guy who sets the world record for fingertip pushups. But it was my good fortune to meet Jack years after his accident. He was in a motorized chair and as far as I knew he had always been disabled.

What drew me to him was his amazing attitude, joy, friendliness, positive attitude, and determination. He was always up for risk-taking adventures. If a group of guys were going bowling, Jack joined us. How does a quadriplegic go bowling, I wondered? I didn't find out until he rolled up to the line.

Jack made me wonder about a lot of things. How is Jack going to babysit my kids while I am on a ministry trip? How does Jack marry Maria and carry his bride down the aisle? How does their honeymoon work? How does he join us for a strenuous hike in the mountains, go scuba diving, play golf, or teach a LAUSD classroom full of elementary kids? I don't know about you, but I'm afraid of a classroom of kids and I'm 6'1" and 200 pounds. The answer is something inside Jack. It's his spirit. He's a champion. He has been able to meet with God in the depths of His suffering and find the strength to persevere.

I've known jack for over thirty years and today he is not only my friend but my hero. When faced with my own obstacles, suffering, confusion, and even frustration with God, I think of what he has endured. I look to his story to help me with my story. I'm not face to face with terrorists or collapsing buildings, I'm facing the great challenges of everyday life. I need role models, people of faith, who show me how to keep going. If you need some encouragement, Jack's story will offer it. I know he'll be an inspiration to you and I hope he will become one of your heroes.

– Pastor Bill Dwyer

Valley Vineyard Christian Fellowship
Reseda, California

❧ **Pride Goes before Destruction** ❧

(Proverbs 16:18)

October 23, 1979, 2:15 p.m.
Fountain Valley Baptist Gymnasium

After graduating from Indiana State University and living in Las Vegas for a couple of years I moved to Fountain Valley, California, to join gymnasts Bee Thoma and Barry Taft on the Athletes in Action team. Their strong faith appealed to me and we had become close friends. The Amateur Athletic Union (AAU) gymnastics invitational was rapidly approaching and I was working overtime to become a qualifier. Jumping up to the six-foot parallel bars, I glanced at the mats below, gauging the distance to the floor. I balanced on one bar and looked over to the other end of the large gymnasium. Bee and Barry were tumbling on the blue 40 x 44 exercise mat.

"Hey, guys," I yelled, "would you take a moment to watch me do a double backflip?"

"Sure, Jack," they replied in unison. Bee moved the blue, eight-foot mat into place, and I double-checked to see that it was secure.

"Okay, Jack. It's ready. Do you need for us to spot you?"

"No," I confidently replied as I reflected on my recent triple backflips off the still rings. "Just watch the over spin." Besides, I said to myself, what was one less flip? The game plan was to start in a handstand, swing up in front of the bars as high as I could go, then push off quickly to the right spinning tightly into a ball without taking a step. I ran the trick over and over in my mind and pictured the landing perfectly.

"Okay, guys," I shouted with pride, "watch this!" Swinging up to the handstand, I paused, then counted to three. "One, two, three - go!" As I swung through the middle of the parallel bars and stretched off to the right, I sensed I was not high enough. I have double vision in my left eye, and I misgauged with my healthy right eye. Deep into the first flip, I pulled my legs in tighter to my chest in hopes that the second flip would turn over. Suddenly I heard a loud crack as my head snapped back violently. I had landed – but how? Apprehension overwhelmed me as I realized that I was on the mat but could not let go of my knees no matter how hard I tried. I felt no pain, yet I had clearly heard a loud snap. Did I break an arm or leg? My body felt numb and I could not move.

Head Coach Paul Tickenoff, a World Games competitor, glanced across the gym with concern and then ran over to me. "I saw that you were really low in the air! Bee said that you told Barry just to spot the overspin." I wanted to tell Paul that I was okay but I knew something was wrong.

"I . . . I think I broke my neck. I can't move!" A gasp came out of their mouths as fear filled their faces. "Coach, I thought I could do a double back but I was too low."

"Are you in pain?

"No, but I can't move."

Paul quickly walked to the telephone and called an ambulance. Seeing tension mounting on Bee's face, I asked him to read Psalm 23.

Bee grabbed his pocket Bible from his backpack and read " . . . though I walk through the valley of the shadow of death, I will fear no evil for You are with me; Your rod and staff comfort me . . . "

I slowly opened my eyes. Could God have taken me to heaven? I felt near the valley of the shadow of death but I had not died. Barry and Bee were still bending over me. Confused, unable to move and barely alive, I could barely breathe. I heard an ambulance siren making its way toward the gym. It screeched to a halt outside. Two doors opened, then slammed. I heard muffled talk and footsteps.

"Hey, Bee," I joked, "this is kind of like the ER reruns!" A male and a female paramedic dressed in blue uniforms stood over me. I felt nervous at the sight of them.

"What happened?" the man asked in a matter-of-fact tone.

Barely able to breathe, I whispered, "I flipped off the parallel bars twice and under spun a double backflip." When he asked if I were able to move, I anxiously retorted, "If I could move, I wouldn't be all balled up in such a contorted position, right?"

After that I tried to keep my cool, but a calm, cool, and collected attitude was impossible. I was a nervous wreck. The female paramedic relayed information on her walkie-talkie. "This is unit five and we've got a red alert. We believe this man has broken his neck. Have a team of doctors ready upon our arrival."

She clipped the walkie-talkie onto her belt and knelt beside me. "Jack, we understand you're feeling anxious, but take some deep breaths. First we're going to check your heart rate. Then we're going to take some blood and monitor your breathing."

As she checked my vital signs, a voice inside me screamed, "You're never going to move again! Why didn't you wear your spotting belt, stupid? Why didn't you ask Bee and Barry to spot you closer?"

However, another voice said, 'Do not blame yourself, Jack. I'm here to comfort you. I am here to help.' I responded to the loving voice. 'Oh, God, if that's You, please forgive me for being so careless and stupid. I'm sorry for not listening to You and asking helpers to catch me. Please turn back the clock!' I cried out in hopes that God would lift me off the mat totally healed. But there was no change. Seconds slowly ticked by. I was losing consciousness. Tests continued on my arms, legs and chests. Then a neck brace was secured. I felt helpless.

When my expensive, brand-new warm-up top was cut off over my loud protests, I felt I had lost control over everything. A clear plastic bag held the ripped remnants. I looked at them and saw my future being tossed away. The man took out a needle and told me to close my eyes so that the test would be accurate. I was to let him know when I felt something. Years of practicing gymnastics had developed in me an acute sense of my body. Surely this would be a simple test.

"When are you going to start? I'm ready for you!" I smiled. Although the paramedic had a grim look on his face, I hoped that I would pass with flying colors.

"Jack, I started two minutes ago! I've been poking your whole body! Didn't you feel it?"

"No, you haven't!" I retorted! "You never started . . . that's a lie! Start now," I demanded. I was sure the problem would soon go away. I'd just get up, take a shower and go home. I closed my eyes. "I feel that," I blurted. "Ouch!"

"Jack, I didn't prick you," he solemnly said.

"Oh, I . . . I meant the one you did a few seconds ago," I half-smiled.

"I haven't started, Jack," he said. "I'm sorry. Your injury is pretty serious. We're going to have to take you in."

It had taken thirteen hard-fought years to get to where I was. Now I had lost control over my muscular body. I tried to pray but instead I heard accusing voices telling me I was a worthless blob. I would never jump up on those parallel bars again or swing on the rings. I thought of Gary Morava, a world-class gymnast, who had broken his neck and died three weeks later. Was I going to follow in his footsteps?

Ironically, only three days earlier I had spoken with Joni Erickson Tada, a quadriplegic who had broken her neck in a diving accident. Since then she had become a well-known author and speaker for the disabled. Bee Thoma and I had gone to a Calvary Chapel worship concert. We arrived to find that hundreds of people had filled the sanctuary so we found a seat near the back on the carpet. We noticed that the bands all dedicated their last songs to Joni Eareckson. Coincidentally, of the two books I had read that year one of them was Joni, Ms. Eareckson's brand new autobiography.

As the evening wrapped up, people left their seats and headed toward me. I felt pretty popular until I turned around to see Joni was right behind me. I introduced myself and shared that I had recently read her book. Joni told me how difficult it had been at first to accept her paralysis. She also told me about a 16-year-old boy who had shown her that God was not the mean person that she thought He was.

She told me with assurance that her accident had actually helped her draw closer to God. Amid the crowd it was as if Joni and I were the only ones left in the chapel. I was talking with one of the most famous Christians about how God brings blessings out of brokenness. I asked her questions about life in a wheelchair. I could hear Joni's words, "Jack, God wants the best for you so be sensitive to his call in whatever you do."

I also recalled that just seven days before my accident a representative for Workmen's Compensation had offered each one of us gymnasts a 100% policy. It would cover us for life for only $15 off our paycheck per month. I had signed on the dotted line.

As the paramedic continued checking my vital signs, I felt like I was in limbo. As my eyes slowly refocused, he assured me that we would be at Fountain Valley Medical Hospital very soon. They carefully transferred me onto a wooden board, buckled it and carried me to the waiting ambulance. I was crying as I heard the doors slam shut. Coach Paul sat by my side and wiped my sweaty head. During that short ride to the hospital I learned what Christ meant about brotherly love. The siren blared as we made our way down the congested streets. Minutes later the driver pulled up to Fountain Valley Medical Hospital. I was near death. I gave one of the paramedics my parents' address and then lapsed into an unconscious state.

I saw a man clothed in a white robe on a grassy knoll. His clear blue eyes communicated love that was pure and powerful. I knew in my spirit that this was no ordinary man—he must be Jesus! He knew everything about the overwhelming plight of paralysis. In his presence I was unafraid and whole . . .

I regained consciousness and heard machines clicking and people talking in the background. A nurse quietly told me that I was in the Fountain Valley Medical Hospital intensive care unit. I had broken my neck and partially severed my spinal cord at cervical three, four and five. My spine was dislocated two and one-quarter inches. She went on to say that I had undergone surgery to reset the vertebra. Still under the effect of the anesthesia, I felt relative peace.

Before drifting back into a drugged sleep, I relived scenes from my childhood in Hinsdale, Illinois. Some were comforting but many were not.

❧ **Part I: Early Challenges** ☙

Majors Clothing Store

Every fall my mother took me to Majors Clothing Store to buy my new school wardrobe. As we pulled up in front, I would tell her that I did not like those clothes.

My mother never said anything as I sullenly followed her inside. She was enthusiastic about her son being the best-dressed kid in school. The bell on the door jangled as we entered the small store. That sound was the opening bell for our seasonal power struggle. It always went something like this:

Round One: I would counter her selection of three pairs of corduroy pants in tan, navy, and black with an emphatic, "No! I want to wear blue jeans like everybody else."

Round Two: Invariably she would buy long-sleeved, pinstriped shirts. I made it clear that I liked pullovers. She said nothing.

Round Three: She always bought all-leather, Stride Rite shoes that resembled Army boots. I desperately wanted to wear tennis shoes.

Without asking my opinion, she would grab three pairs of dark blue socks and then march to the checkout counter while I already had one foot out the door. As we left, the final bell on the door signaled that I was down for the count. Although Mom might have won on the outside, on the inside I was wearing a pullover shirt, blue jeans and tennies. I always hoped never to set foot into Majors again but the next year it was déjà vu all over again.

Florida

I did have one very fond memory of our family visiting my grandparents in Clearwater Beach, Florida, during Easter vacations. It was still cold where we lived in Hinsdale, Illinois, but when our plane landed in Florida, palm trees swayed in the warm, gentle breeze. Seagulls cawed overhead. The temperature was 80° and I felt like we been transported to a magical place. My sister Jeanne--older by two years-- and I looked forward to those Florida vacations when we were both in elementary school. We enjoyed going to the beach, horseback riding and playing miniature golf.

Every morning Mom would smear Jeanne and me with Tropicana suntan lotion before we walked to a secluded, private beach carrying sack lunches, pails and shovels. Occasionally we'd bring a bag of Wonder Bread for the seagulls. We would toss our clogs and lunches on the sand and run into the warm, aqua water. As Jeanne and I jumped up and down over the waves, we laughed with giddy pleasure in a carefree world of our own.

Sand dollars covered with ruddy fur littered the ocean floor. I would dig far down into the sand to find 6-inch crabs. Scooping them up with my shovel, I would toss them into the awaiting "Roman Coliseum Arena" for a fight to the finish! The winner would be set free. Although the loser never died, he often lost his claws. Afterwards I'd let the crustacean gladiators race to freedom across the hot, white sand. Ever since then I have been drawn to the warm, turquoise water of the Gulf . . .

Screech went the hospital bed. I was immediately catapulted back to the present. I was not on the white, sandy Florida beach. Instead, I was covered with white sheets and surrounded by the white walls of the Intensive Care Ward. It was midnight and a nurse turned me on my side to prevent pressure sores. Tubes of every type, length, and color entered and exited me. I looked like the *Six Million Dollar Man*! To my right I could hear the steady *bleep, bleep* of the heart machine. Overhead from a clear plastic bag, glucose dripped ever so slowly via a tube into my right arm. *Swoosh, swoosh* came the sound from the noisy air–breathing machine. In a morphine haze I drifted in and out of consciousness. Like a dying man, my life flashed before my eyes in the six-hour intervals of being turned onto my back, onto my side, onto my stomach, onto my other side . . .

Second Grade

I will never, ever forget second grade--the worst year of my young life. It was a year of total humiliation and isolation. Until my paralysis, second grade had been the low point of my entire life.

My only good second-grade memory is of Jennifer Moody who sat in front of me. I will never forget sitting down at my wooden desk, putting my supplies on the tray and peeking around to see her name. I slouched farther down into my new Stride Rite shoes. I mentally said her name, Jennifer Moody. Then I got a glimpse of her face. My heart pitter-pattered and then skipped a beat. She was beautiful! I was in a trance still thinking about Jennifer when I suddenly heard the teacher call my name. She told me in front of the entire class that she had already called my name several times. Embarrassed, I admitted that I wasn't listening. In fact, I never heard anything the teacher said during the rest of the day.

One evening I almost got up the nerve to call Jennifer on the phone. The more I thought about it, the more scared I felt. Besides, what if my dad picked up the phone to make a call and I was on the line? I would have frozen like an icicle and broken in half! Jennifer Moody was the only thing that made that year bearable. I never told my family about her and Jennifer never knew that I was smitten with her.

What I hated about second grade was how poorly I did in every subject but physical education. I can't just blame my poor performance on my infatuation with Jennifer Moody. I had difficulty paying attention—period. Like many boys, I doodled in class. I revered Leonardo da Vinci. Multi-talented, he had sculpted *David* and *Pieta*, painted the *Last Supper* and the *Mona Lisa*, had designed bridges and invented helicopters. I tried to imitate his artwork. When Mrs. Finkelstein walked by, I would quickly shove my "Leonardo" drawings into my desk. After she walked away, I would take out my sketchpad and continue drawing. One day she caught me and demanded, "So, Jack, how did the Native Americans come to the United states?"

I thought for a moment and took a guess. "Six times nine equals twenty three." The class burst out laughing. I put my head down in shame. How was I ever going to impress Jennifer if I was a dunce?

Monroe Elementary School used a reading program called SRA. The color of the book coordinated with the reading level. Green was the highest level and purple was the lowest. I was in the purple group. While most of the kids were reading full stories, I was still reading *Jack and Jill*. I felt ashamed and extremely stressed about not doing well in school. I angrily lashed out at myself and even at God. Among other things, I lit gasoline in the backyard and burned a paper with my name on it. I blew up trashcans with cherry bombs and ignited GI Joes by the side of the house. I was finally diagnosed with dyslexia and in third grade I was pulled out of reading to go to a special class. Further humiliation!

Another incident added to my shame and low self-esteem. One afternoon I stopped by the dime store on my way home from school for some candy. I stared greedily at what seemed to me like every candy in the world: Hot Tamales, Dots and my favorite--M&M's. I didn't have enough money so I slipped the M&M's into my right pocket. I was about to walk out the door when I glanced down. I couldn't believe it! I thought the M&M's were in my right pocket, but to my dismay, the bag was on my right shoe. The store manager yelled, "Hey, what are you doing stealing that candy?" He walked over to me, grabbed my right ear and used it to pull me behind the counter. I was shaking in my Stride Rite shoes.

A couple of customers were in line so I had to wait a few minutes. I thought maybe I could make a run for it out the door but then I figured it would be worse if he caught me. I would only be in deeper trouble. So I stood behind the counter waiting for the store manager to make a decision. When the line of customers was finished, he demanded in an angry tone, "So what were you doing stealing that candy?"

"I don't know. The candy was just there on my foot!" The store manager stared at me. He knew I was lying. I lowered my head as he told me what I already knew; I was in a lot of trouble. He took me into his office and sat me down next to him. He called the police. He wanted to take me down to the station but I think they told him to call my parents instead. He told me that he thought I had learned my lesson but he called my mother anyway.

I walked home very slowly. When I got to the door my mother looked angry. "Wait till your father comes home! Go down to your room." Later that evening I heard my mom talking to Dad. Then I heard his footsteps coming down the hallway. He knocked on my door, walked in and looked at me sternly. "Your mother told me what you did at the store today." I didn't say anything. "I'm disappointed in you, Son!" He was holding a wooden board with his fraternity logo branded in the middle. He told me to pull down my pants and lean over the bed. It seemed like I had that logo branded on my rear for a week. I could hardly sit down!

The interminable second grade school year finally ended. Mrs. Finkelstein handed out the report cards. She put mine down on my desk and I slowly opened it and looked at my grades. Reading: F, Math: F, Writing: F, Science: D-, Social Studies: D, and Physical Education: A. I sank down into my seat in despair. Everybody else was jumping up and down because they had good grades. All I could think of was showing my parents my dumb report card. I stuffed it far down in the bottom of my backpack. As I rounded the corner toward home, I decided to get rid of it. I saw an old oak tree with a giant hole near the bottom. Looking left and right to make sure that no one could see me, I took the report card out and stuffed it deep into the center of the tree. Then I walked home.

My mom didn't believe me when I told her that I had never received a report card. I sullenly confessed what I had done. She ordered me to go and get it right that instant. I walked back to the old oak tree, pulled out my report card and opened it up. To my relief, there was a giant hole in the middle. I think a squirrel had eaten it. I went home and gave it to Mom. Because the inside of my report card was gone, my mother couldn't see the grades. I expected her to ask me what they were and I thought I could just make them up. But she didn't ask. Instead she ordered me to go back to school and get another one. When he came home from work, Dad read each grade out loud. "I feel for you, Son. I never did well in school. But you're going to have to repeat second grade."

Not only did I not have summer vacation, but I had to retake second grade in summer school. Because I had been diagnosed with dyslexia, Mrs. Schwisow tutored me in reading after school. I looked out her front window every afternoon as my classmates played basketball. My self-esteem was at an all-time low. Plus in the fall I would start third grade in the low reading group. I felt worthless and stupid. Wearing Mom's newly-bought clothes from Majors, unable to make a friend, I felt like nothing EVER was going to go right. I felt like a real loser.

To pass the time away some lonely afternoons I would climb the backyard maple tree—thirty-five feet high! I went from branch to branch, stretching one leg upwards in a splits position then grabbing another branch. After thirty minutes I'd be at the top near a bird's nest. I could overlook the rooftop and see into the front yard. We also had an apple tree in the far backyard. I'd climb my way to the top where I could pick the best apples, sweeter than honey. I ate three or four at a time.

One day Mom came out the back door looking for me because I hadn't done my homework and also because she was going to give me a piano lesson, which I hated! When she called me, I didn't say anything hoping she'd leave and I would get out of my homework and the piano lesson. It was difficult balancing up at the top of the tree. A branch cracked and she looked up and saw me. The good thing was that my mother saw me swinging from limb to limb and doing the splits. She changed my life by signing me up for age-group gymnastics at the high school on Wednesday evenings. For many years Mom drove me back and forth to the gym and supported me during gymnastic meets behind the bleachers. This was a sacrifice of love because she was also busy teaching piano, organ and Bible studies as well as running the household.

My neighbor, Steve Shepard, was in my gymnastics age-group that met at the high school. He lived a couple of blocks away and was also in my class at school. Kids stared at him because one eye had a lazy muscle that caused his pupil to wander off center. I had always admired Steve because he didn't let that bother him.

Thinking about Steve's wandering eye reminded me of a horrible accident I had when I was thirteen involving my left eye. In August of 1968 my parents sent me on a Boy Scout trip to Quetico, Canada. I really didn't want to go because I was a city boy and The Monkees rock group was playing in downtown Chicago that week . Thirty other Boy Scouts and I climbed aboard the big Greyhound bus with our sleeping bags, backpacks and dried fruit. The trip took eight hours. We finally arrived at our first destination, Ely, Minnesota, at 6 a.m. Evergreen trees loomed over me, and the air was cold and crisp. The surroundings scared and overwhelmed me. Up in this country, salmon, blue gill and pike could be caught in the river streams. We stopped to buy multi-hooked bait, called 'remoras,' to secure to our fly rods. Remora are a type of suckerfish commonly used as bait to attract bigger fish. Paul Avril, a neighbor, bought a couple of hooks so he would have a better chance.

The next day our Boy Scout leader, Mr. Elmendorf, took us by foot and by canoe into the wilderness, upstream where the fishing was good. Paul and I had a brief lunch and waded out to the middle of the stream to fish. His lanky remora dangled from the fish reel. I watched from a distance but I couldn't see whether he was getting any bites. I moved closer, but Paul didn't hear me over the roaring water. As I jumped from rock to rock, Paul cast back his line and his hook hit me in the face.

"Jack, are you all right?" Paul shouted. I really didn't know what he meant. Mr. Elmendorf had seen the accident and ran over to assist me. He told me not to move because I had a fishhook in my eye. He clipped the line and helped me back to the sandy beach. I felt afraid but I was even more worried about what I looked like with a fishhook lodged in my eye. I raised my hand toward my face and a voice said, "Jack, don't do that!" I put my hand down and lay still. By the time a park ranger arrived three hours later, my left eye was hemorrhaging badly. The fishhook had lodged itself in my left pupil, cheek, eyebrow and ear. Even the ranger said he had not seen such a gory sight in some time.

A medical evacuation plane landed in a nearby lake, and I was canoed out and lifted on board. Off I went with Mr. Elmendorf to Ely Mercy Hospital in Minnesota. The operation lasted for four hours. As I awoke, I heard the muted voice of a nurse. The doctor had had difficulty removing the fishhook from the pupil and their unit was not capable of completing the operation. I was to be flown down to Chicago for further surgeries. Dad and Mom were notified by the Minnesota hospital staff that I was being transferred. Early the next morning, I was whisked onto an air cargo plane and rushed to Chicago's Presbyterian St. Luke's Hospital. As I was being wheeled flat into the operating room with both eyes bandaged, I was comforted at hearing my parents' reassuring voices.

I imagined their fearful faces as they remembered their smiling son waving from the Greyhound bus only to return on an air ambulance stretcher. "We love you and we're going to be right by your side to help in any way we can," Dad said. He would say those same words almost a decade later.

The operation seemed successful; the embedded hook was removed from the cornea and pupil. I lay in the hospital unable to see for the next three weeks. Gauze covered both eyes so that the right eye would not get stronger than the left. I was like a blind person, unable to go anywhere without assistance. I felt helpless and depressed. After the third week I was told that my left eye had begun to hemorrhage and blood had rushed to the cornea. I would have surgery as soon as possible to remove my left eye. I shook all over. I thought of a classmate Chip Heady whose eye had been removed after a superball accident. The other kids treated him like an outcast. Was I going to become the next Chip Heady? I was angry with God. I thought I had been dealt enough blows for a kid.

My parents rushed to the hospital with Pastor Nelson who asked if I minded if he prayed for me. I managed to mutter an okay.

"Lord, we don't understand why Jack and his parents are experiencing this, but we ask for a miracle out of your goodness and that Christ would dwell in his heart." Pastor Nelson then asked if I wanted to receive Christ into my heart and I said that I would. At that exact moment the most beautiful yet terrifying thing happened. I thought the nurse had removed the eye patches from my eyes because I could see a small, faraway light. It grew larger and larger like a street lamp and then it was the size of the sun. The light was so bright and intense that I called out in fear, yet at the same time I felt a cleansing within my left eye.

"I felt like something happened to my eye," I cried out joyfully. A skeptical nurse humored me by removing the patch from my left eye. The hemorrhaging was gone! I still felt like I was looking at the noonday sun but in reality all the lights were turned off in the room. Moments later Dr. Perry checked my eye with her mirror and told me that my eye must have healed itself and that I was a lucky boy. Lucky? I knew my eye couldn't have healed itself! The miracle reminded me of Saul blinded by a bright light on the road to Damascus only to regain his sight three days later.

Nevertheless, I was left with double vision in that eye and it wandered to the left. For the next year I had to wear an eye patch on my right eye to strengthen the left one and go to therapy in downtown Chicago. At junior high school students stared at me in the halls and formed a wide swath around me. I was treated like another Chip Heady. I became introverted and unable to share my feelings. I experienced sudden bursts of anger and I stayed in my room for long periods of time. It was difficult for my parents as well. Each day Mom spent half an hour trying to make both eyes track simultaneously. They never did. I hated having double vision because I couldn't tell which image was the true one. My classmates treated me like a pariah. I felt totally handicapped—a real *Charlie Brown*.

When I awoke in the ICU, I felt the weight of too many handicaps: dyslexia, double vision and now paralysis. I kept thinking, "God won't give me more than I can handle." My view of a loving God was all screwed up. Having faith wasn't necessarily gong to guarantee that all my problems would be washed away.

❧ **Part 2: Flip Flops** ☙

Eighth Grade

As I began eighth grade, I became even more involved in gymnastics, not only at the gym but at home as well. I loved to do back-bends, splits and cartwheels in the backyard. Inside, I would run down the hallway, pick up speed and kick my feet overhead to land in a handstand.

My neighbor with a lazy eye, Steve Shepard, lived a couple of blocks away, and was in my gymnastics class. I now felt comfortable with him since my own eye accident. I had felt self-conscious about my wandering left eye. He had accepted his own visual disability and encouraged me to talk about mine.

We enjoyed challenging each other doing flips, cartwheels and floor exercises. Looking back, I realize how unusual it is for two boys that age to be so supportive of each other. We practiced flip-flops and handstand pushups on our back lawns. We spent many hours tumbling and practicing strength moves. Steve eventually became better in floor exercise events while I was better on the parallel bars. My small body could bend and swing high on the parallel bars during twists and turns. I won first place in the district and felt like I had at last found a place to belong.

We both loved the trampoline. Steve could bounce high in the air doing doubles as well as double twisting back flips. Together we would jump onto the trampoline and double bounce each other high in the air. On our way home we would play on the old junior high school fire escapes. We climbed like spiders up to the top and then slid down. We continued spurring each other on through the summer months. Steve gradually became better at flipping and I got stronger in pushups and sit-ups. Our goal at the end of summer was to be on the gymnastics team at Hinsdale Central High School.

High School Gymnastics

To me, gymnastics was kinetic art. I loved the beauty of gymnasts flying in the air, twisting and landing on their feet. I could feel the strength of the still rings performer holding the Iron Cross. I felt the gymnast flying gracefully around the high bar. I fantasized about being in his place. Hinsdale Central High School boasted academic and sports excellence. They held records for state, national, and Olympics in tennis, wrestling, swimming and gymnastics for many decades. It was a dream to represent the school. I gazed at the large board on the wall of the gymnastics room. For twenty years familiar gymnasts had left their marks in various events such as pommel horse and high bar. Gazing up at the wall of champions, I quietly said to myself, "That's my goal."

One of my favorite memories was the day I tried out for the freshman team, along with forty others. We were interviewed, not by name, but by the number of push-ups, sit-ups and chin-ups we could do as well as by our flexibility and the skills we exhibited. Slender, balding Coach Bull was in charge of the freshman team. With an impressive record of 151 wins, 32 losses and 17 ties, he was the catalyst for the varsity team's success. After watching me do handstand pushups, splits, small dance moves, cartwheels and a front flip, Coach Bull said that he thought I was going to be a great gymnast. I did not tell him about my double vision for fear that he would not let me be on the team. I had thought I would never amount to anything because of my dyslexia and double vision until Coach Bull's words of encouragement rang in my ears. For the first time I thought that maybe I could be somebody great!

Next was Steve's chance to show Coach Bull what he could do. Steve performed leg splits in all three directions. He did a cartwheel, rounded off and executed a backhand spring. When the coach asked where he had learned all that, Steve told him that we sparred at each other's homes. When Coach told Steve that he, too, was on the freshman team, we were both ecstatic.

'Frosh' gymnastics was not an exciting sport to watch. We fell a lot, forgot our routines and could manage only a few skills. The meets were off in a corner where hardly anybody could find us. The wood floors were cold and the temperature was brisk. Nevertheless, the gymnasts' mothers came to cheer us on. Mine was proud of me. Sitting on hard bleachers, she spurred me on for countless hours. I realize in retrospect that she could have done other things during that time.

I had a long way to go in beginning gymnastics. I scored 2.5 out of 10.0 on the parallel bars, a 1.9 on the floor exercise, and a 2.1 on the still rings. Steve scored higher on floor exercise—a respectable 4.1. It was not world-class gymnastics, but it was fun!

Later that year, I got up the nerve to challenge senior Bob Anderson, the top-rated gymnast in Illinois, to a V-Sit contest on the parallel bars. The object was to hold my legs up off the bars at a 45-degree angle and then raise them to my face with my arms supporting my weight. Bob looked at me as if I were crazy. He was a BMOC—big man on campus—meaning all the girls loved him. He was bright, handsome and a state All-American and captain of the varsity gym team. He walked away from me with a smirk and told some of his senior buddies what I had said. I felt like a fool. Was I really going to beat Bob Anderson?

Seconds later he came back and retorted, "Sure, I'll challenge you. When do you want to have this contest?"

"Why not now?" I nervously asked, trying to look poised and confident. Inside I was a bundle of nerves. It was David versus Goliath. I saw myself as never having much potential. I was small, introverted and had never done well in school. I thought all my friends were more talented than I was, that they could learn skills faster, get better grades and date the best-looking girls. Nevertheless, this was my chance to show them who was best.

Upper and lower classmen came over to watch. I overheard mumbled comments like, "No way!" Everyone gathered around and watched. Freshmen and sophomores rooted for me; the upperclassman shouted for Bob. He and I jumped onto opposite ends of the bars. The contest was to lift our legs up to our heads and hold them as long as possible. I glanced across at Bob. He looked strong. My legs hovered in the air between my arms. "35, 45, 50 seconds . . . " Everybody cheered. My legs began to drop below my face, but Bob's legs looked strong. My face was sweaty with exhaustion; his was composed. I had to hold on. This was my chance to get back at all those seniors who mocked us freshmen for being so skinny and weak. Seconds went by . . . 51, 52, 53, 55 . . . 57. Out of the corner of my eye I saw Bob's face showing strain. His legs began to drop and then they fell.

"I did it! I beat him!" I yelled. Sweat dripped from my forehead as my legs slowly dropped to balance on the parallel bars. I had gone 60 seconds! Bob and the seniors walked back to the mats with their tails between their legs. It was a victory that significantly boosted my confidence.

Freshman year came to a close. Our team won the state competition and I placed first in the parallel bars. I worked hard over the break and enrolled in evening programs and summer camps. Pushing my body to its limits had paid off. I trained hard and was willing to take some risks. Gymnastics was rapidly becoming more difficult than I thought.

Hinsdale Central had two of the best varsity coaches anywhere, Coach Omi and Coach Canino, but it was Coach Canino we feared. Each day after school we were to report to the tiny gym at precisely 3 p.m. Coach Canino then shut the double doors. If a gymnast didn't make it inside those wooden doors by exactly 3 p.m., he was off the team, even if he was an all-American. Coach oversaw the elite varsity team. Once a sergeant in the Marines, he was a strong, bull-headed man. If you tried to just 'chat' with him, he would send a disdainful look that said, "Hey, Bud, you're wasting my time. Do you have a question regarding gymnastics?"

Coach wore a tight Hinsdale Central v-neck shirt—his arm muscles bulging out the sleeves—and a pair of red warm-up pants. His hair was always perfectly combed and his demeanor conveyed confidence. A story circulated that he was once demonstrating to some varsity gymnasts how to lift weights over his head when he tore a bicep right off the bone. To the astonishment of his gymnasts, he did not even flinch but continued to lift the weights. Coach Canino held weekly meetings and updated us on team and individual scores. These were typed and then averaged against the top 10 teams in the district and state. His trite maxims inspired us to excel: "Today is tomorrow's yesterday," "Tomorrow will never come," and "No guts, no glory."

The highlight of the school year was to qualify for the state gymnastics finals. Channel 9 in Chicago televised the meet live. Individual winners won beautiful trophies and the championship team won a gold plaque. Top college scouts from Arizona, Pennsylvania, Oregon and Indiana State Universities were all there. My goal was to make the state finals and to receive a full scholarship.

At gym meets, Hinsdale Central was much like an army unit. We marched out in unison. Dry-cleaned uniforms covered toned, muscled bodies. We were a fearful sight for the opposing team. We worked together to form a team that no other high school could beat; in fact, 75% of the college teams couldn't beat us. Teachers, friends and students we didn't even know all respected us. At school assemblies we were recognized by name. Store owners would say hello and the local newspaper wrote long articles about us accompanied by photographs.

We practiced five days a week from 3 to 6 p.m. Saturdays were special treats—a full day of weight lifting and running 5 miles around the hot track. We ran the stairs inside the huge gym and outside in the cold, blustery, winter wind. Afterwards, I would drag my exhausted body home. Sometimes I would fall asleep at the dinner table. Once, my face landed right in the spaghetti!

One late afternoon I was attempting a full giant swing on the horizontal bar. If you've been to the zoo to see the chimpanzees swinging round and round, you'll know what the giant is. I was terrified because the bar was more than eight feet off the ground and, to add to that, swinging in a handstand made me feel like I was touching the ceiling. Coaches Omi and Canino required mastering this skill before graduating to the varsity team. I jumped up, pushed my body nervously to the handstand while both coaches watched below. I swung through, hitting the handstand, and pushed away towards the bottom, when suddenly my grip loosened. "Aaahhh," I yelled. I flew off the bar like a dart, my hands striking the mat below.

Coaches Omi and Canino ran over as I lay dazed. When I attempted to push off the mat, I could not get up right away. My right wrist dangled. I slowly got to my feet, feeling faint. I was rushed to the hospital for x-rays. My wrist had been fractured in three places and my arm was nearly paralyzed. I was sidelined. I watched all my peers improve in their gymnastic skills ahead of me. It was a long and difficult road back.

After I recovered and senior year approached, I decided to specialize in the still rings in hopes of making the varsity team. By working out four hours after school every day, I was able to land a spot on the still rings team. It was not my first choice because it was the all-around gymnast who received the glory--and the full scholarship. By the end of high school, I had improved enough to score eight out of ten. However, that was not good enough to make it to the state finals. I would not be listed on the Wall of Champions, nor would I receive a college scholarship. Nevertheless, some time after my accident, an annual 'Jack Fischer Courage and Perseverance Award' plaque was added to the wall.

I had another *Charlie Brown* episode the day of the ACT (American College Testing) exam, the all-important achievement test to determine college admissions. Just before time to leave, our dachshund Fritz bit my thumb. It bled profusely for an hour, making me late for the test. I couldn't do anything right!

The proctor ushered me to my seat and informed me that I had sixty minutes to complete the exam. I stared at the questions. None of the answers looked like the right one. The clock on the wall ticked louder with each question. No way was I going to finish this test! Before I knew it, the proctor announced, "Time. Put your pencils down." I could hear people chatting all around me saying how easy the test was for them and how quickly they had finished.

I knew I had flunked this one badly. How could one exam determine where I would go to college? It seemed extremely unfair. Weeks later I received my national ranking. As I expected, I scored at the bottom, only good enough for a junior college. To tell the town of Hinsdale that I was going to the local 'JC' would be humiliating. My self-esteem plummeted below sub-level. Steve Shepherd called me to tell he was going to Penn State.

Indiana State University Gymnastics

In spite of my low ACT score, my lucky day came when the Admissions Office at Indiana State University called to say that I was admitted for one semester on academic probation. I later learned that ISU Coach Roger Council had pulled some strings; otherwise, I would not remotely have been accepted with my low scores.

I was on my way down Interstate 70 to Indiana State University, land of the Hoosiers. This was basketball country, where Larry Bird was as popular as Governor Bowan. Terre Haute—comprised of farmers, small businessmen and college students—was much different from Hinsdale. Nearly everyone wore OshKosh overalls and talked about farm life. Stores lining the town's main street were as old as the Wabash River. The movie theater only showed pornography and there was just one fast food restaurant.

Within hours of arriving I was already homesick for Chicago. I missed home-cooked meals, friends and familiar stores. People talked different, looked different and walked different. Winter nights brought high winds and deep snow drifts. Crossing the one-mile campus could take up to twenty minutes. Nevertheless, I soon realized that all the lamenting in the world would not do me any good. I had come here to get an education and sharpen my gymnastic skills.

The Sycamore Gymnastics Program had been under the direction of Coach Roger Council for the past thirteen years. He had built an empire of excellence. In 1963 the team finished its season with a 3-5 record. The following year ISU was above the .500 mark, finishing 5-4-2. Then in 1967 the team was 9-3, placing third in the Nationals. Council, an All-American gymnast himself, was also a glutton for punishment. He did not care that I carried a full academic load and had dyslexia. He had paid good money to recruit me; therefore, he expected a champion with uncompromised dedication.

Practices spanned eleven months, six days a week, three to six hours a day. This was the big leagues. How could I manage to compete and get passing grades at the same time? Not only that, but most of the guys were recruited for being all-around gymnasts, competing in all six events. Because I did not have enough talent, my only option was to specialize in the still rings that I really enjoyed. As the term implies, the name of the game was to keep the ring still. If the performer unintentionally let the rings swing back and forth even once, points were deducted from the final score. Still rings was a man's event. Football players loved to show off as their girlfriends watched, but the still rings was more than a muscle event. The gymnast had to be flexible to endure 360° swings that could pull arms out of sockets. I was attracted to the challenge. My motto had always been 'The harder the challenge, the better.'

In gymnastics each routine is made up of a set of skills consisting of easy, medium and difficult parts called A, B and C moves. Each routine requires four A parts (one point), three B parts (two points), and one or more C parts (up to three points) on a scale of zero to ten with ten being perfect and zero being poor. A deduction of up to one full point out of ten is made if the gymnast slips or sways more than once. The judge can award a tenth of a point or more for originality. A skill performed with virtuosity—a particular flair that separates the gymnast from the rest—receives an additional tenth of a point or more.

Taking a risk is another way the gymnast can receive extra tenths of a point; for example, the high bar is known for risky routines. The gymnast flings his body up in the air and dismounts, spinning many times. I revered ISU senior Tom Morgan's 'C' strength move called "The Gunny." He started from a hanging position and then pulled his body with straight arms up to the Iron Cross. For full credit, Tom had to hold the move for three seconds. A hush came over the crowd as though we were witnessing super-human strength. In time I vowed not only to perform the "Gunny," but to do so with flair.

National Gymnastic Championship

After four years of dedicated practice, I was a finalist in the National Gymnastics Championship hosted by Arizona State University. It was 7:30 PM and I could feel the excitement of the crowd. The announcer's voice came over the loudspeaker, "Welcome to the Finals of the National Gymnastics Championships. Tonight at Arizona State Sports Center are the top gymnasts in the United States, if not in the world. Let's give them a big hand for their hard work." The crowd roared in appreciation. Someone once said that gymnastics is the most difficult sport because it incorporates all the sports into one.

As the national anthem played and the flag rose, I felt proud to be a gymnast and proud to be an American. I felt like Superman ready to show off my super-human strength. I sensed the electricity in the air. I could hardly wait to jump up on the still rings above the spectators in the huge sports center. I marched back with my team to our chairs.

"Hey, brother Jack!" I turned my head and saw Dad and Mom in the balcony. I loved my dad. What a support he was! I used to try handstands in the hallway, crashing into walls and into furniture and Dad did not seem to mind. How he ever put up with me, I'll never know! Mom cried for joy, proud to finally see her son achieve his ultimate goal. I was proud to be a Fischer. I turned and waved to them with tears in my eyes.

The still rings event was quickly approaching. I had sacrificed months of my life with broken bones, stitches and concussions to make it to the nationals. I remembered all those countless hours of practicing—sweating like a hog, lifting weights, running, and going over routines. Dressed in my shiny, blue uniform with the white insignia of ISU, I assured Coach, who had encouraged me for four years, that I would do my best. In the background I could hear other teams cheering for their teammates. Directly above me in the stands were hundreds of ISU supporters who had been bussed across the country to cheer our team on. Insecurities gone, I felt ready to rip those still rings apart. I was Samson ready to pull down the pillars before the Philistine army! Nevertheless, I cringed at the talent I was up against. My old high school teammate Doug Wood from Iowa State rated number one in the nation all year. Louisiana State strongman Jim Blush. Olympian Peter

Korman. World Games record holder Kurt Thomas. Pan-American Games winner Bart Conner.

I stood up, pulled off my sleek, polyester Indiana State warm-up jacket and slipped on the white form pants. I slowly walked to the still rings event. I watched Doug Wood before me. His routine flowed ending with a perfect pike doubled back flip. His score was 9.8!

Teammate John Golbeck encouraged me as the loudspeaker blared, "Up next for Indiana State University, Jack Fischer." The television lights shone brightly on my sleek, blue and white competition uniform. I walked to the chalk tray and placed my sweaty hands in the chalk to prevent them from slipping. I mentally ran over my routine in stop-action photos from beginning to the end, landing on my feet.

Assistant coach Rick Danley assured me that he would call me out of the double back. We both smiled and then I tightened my cowhide handgrips. Signaling to the head judge, I walked slowly onto the slick, spongy mat. He nodded for me to go ahead. Rick came up behind me and hoisted me up to the seven-foot high rings. The audience, teammates, Coach Council and my parents all watched in anticipation. I grabbed the chalk-filled rings and tried not to think about the severe shoulder strain I had suffered attempting the move earlier in the year. The gunny was the most difficult of the strength moves. With Rick's help, I adjusted my hands in a false grip over the rings. As he walked away, I felt my body's dead weight hanging from my hands, arms and shoulders. Grunting and clinging tightly, I inched my way up to the cross. The pressure and strain were unbelievable. *Click, click* went the cameras.

I felt no shoulder pain or strain as my adrenaline flowed. Holding the cross with confidence, I proceeded to swing backwards around in a dislocate, rotating my shoulders backwards and up via a shoot to the handstand. The rings became still as I swung to the bottom and up to the handstand again. I could perform this skill forward and backward in my sleep. Next would be a series of strength moves. I was becoming winded.

The audience *oohed* and *aahed* as I lowered slowly from the handstand to hold my body parallel to the floor in a Maltese cross then lifted my upper body into a seated position to form an L cross. I finished my last routine as the cameras clicked and people clapped. Dislocating my shoulders to a back lever, I kicked up above the rings, swinging my legs forward and lifting my body to an 'L' hold. I paused to catch my breath. It was almost over. With sweaty concentration I tightened my grip and pushed away fifteen feet up from the bottom to the handstand. Then, pulling my body up as hard as I could, I threw the rings away and flipped backwards twice in a pike position. I heard complete silence. Had I landed on my feet? Suddenly, amid loud cheers I found myself standing straight and upright on my feet. I had stuck the dismount without taking a single step!

A jubilant voice rang out over the loudspeaker, "Scoring a 9.55 in second place from ISU: Jack Fischer." I was amazed. My dream had come true. I stepped up onto the victory platform, an All-American, second in the nation! My score was good enough to push ISU into a tie with rival Oklahoma State for the team title--434.475 points to 434.475! Only once before in NCAA gymnastics championships history had two teams tied for the national title. Teammate Kurt Thomas won the all-around title. The team was awarded a large, shiny gold-embossed plaque. I received an individual medal and a team gold medal.

I had drooled over those awards for years. Now they were mine! God had not let me down. I felt like I was in heaven. Could life get any better? I had finally found my niche. I was delirious with joy. The whole nation had watched me on ABC; I felt famous. This was the final meet of my thirteen-year career and I was in the spotlight. ABC's television cameras had focused in on the action; newspaper photographers' flash-bulbs had lit up the still rings event. Afterwards journalists wrote as fast as I could speak. I was an All-American and a member of the ISU National team! I felt like God was on my side now and I could succeed at anything.

Indiana State University had won the nationals and the team was on a high. Back home champagne flowed and steaks sizzled. A parade honored us; our picture was on the front page of the University news-paper. The next day as my teammates and I were sitting around the gym basking in our glory, I had the idea that our team could 'streak' that Saturday evening. I might have been shy, but when it came to partying I was the leader!

"Are you crazy?" my roommate John said. "What if we get caught? Our asses will be red!" I laughed at the thought of our butts getting tanned but the thought of streaking kept running through my mind. Everyone was up for it and agreed to meet me at my dorm at 9 o'clock. Saturday night arrived and they all were waiting for me to tell them how we were going to pull this off. I told them we would walk over to the tennis courts, strip down behind the bushes, make a run through the crowd and meet up back at the bushes.

Someone, however, had tipped off the crowd and they all started hooting, hollering and clapping in anticipation. We took off our shirts, shorts and tennis shoes and began running through the crowd. Someone put his foot out and tripped me sending my dorm keys flying through the legs of the crowd. While I was on the ground with scraped knees and elbows, the crowd kicked my keys farther and farther away. I crawled faster trying to find them while my teammates hid behind the building. I finally was able to retrieve my keys. "What are you doing, Jack? We're freezing!" After I told the team what had happened, they laughingly chided me. We made it back to the bushes and put our clothes on.

The next day I thought everything was fine until John came back from breakfast holding a school newspaper. "Jack, you won't believe what's on the front page." I stared at a giant picture of our team in the nude running through the crowd. The caption read, "National Team Caught Streaking!" My jaw dropped.

"Oh, no. What are we going to do?"

"You'd better hope and pray that coach doesn't see this!"

That afternoon we all sat in a circle in the gym stretching our legs. Coach Council walked in holding up a newspaper and wearing a stern look. "Whose idea was this? I am disgraced and ashamed of you. You made me look like a fool not only in front of the University but in front of the nation!" Nobody spoke up. I thought my friends would point a finger at me but they did not. Coach stood there in wordless disgust. It was a long and quiet workout.

The Thrill of Victory and the Agony of Defeat

My mind drifted back to another challenge I had overcome. Actually, it had ended up being the thrill of victory followed by the agony of defeat, but for a few brief months I had basked in the thrill.

During the month following my placement in the Nationals, I was enjoying summer vacation on my parents' sofa when an idea occurred to me: Maybe I could get my name in the Guinness World Book of Records. I flipped through the pages until I came to push-ups. The record for fingertip push-ups was 140 in 80 seconds. I thought I could do that easily until I realized after trying that I was so out of shape that I could not even get to 50 but I was not going to give up. I still had 11 units to complete before receiving my bachelor's degree.

Back at ISU I headed for the gym after classes each day. Re-conditioning was slow—sixty-five push-ups, then seventy-five. I began to doubt that breaking the record was within reach. Nevertheless, I practiced every afternoon as the clock ticked away and sweat dripped off my face. Two months later I was getting closer—125 finger pushups in ninety seconds. I thought I could break the record.

I told none of my teammates or friends because I was afraid they would laugh at me for trying something so outlandish. The one man I confided in was sports information director Ed McGee. When I told him my dream and that I had pumped out 125 in ninety seconds, Ed was impressed. I had a burning desire to be the best. With daily practices I came within fifteen fingertip push-ups of breaking the record. I hoped adrenaline would take me over the top.

Beverly Waites at Guinness told me that in order for the record to count officially, I had to have a notarized log signed by two witnesses, have local newspaper and TV coverage of the event, authenticity of push-ups by a qualified person, and the correct fingertip pushup method indicated by the Guinness.

I finally felt confident enough to tell some of my close teammates. They showed up at the gym to watch me challenge the existing record. Some questioned my ability while others supported me. I, myself, concentrated on breaking the record. I balanced on my fingertips, my body in push-up position in front of the TV camera and the press.

The timekeeper looked at the stopwatch. "Are you ready, Jack?"

"Ready as I'll ever be!" I confidently said. Nevertheless, I began to doubt whether I would make it past 50. I pumped out 40 push-ups in 30 seconds. I had to pick it up. At this rate I would only do 100 in 80 seconds. My reputation was on the line. Pumping into high gear, I contracted my muscles even tighter as I dropped to the floor, each time my chest touching the scorekeeper's hand.

Seventy seconds raced by. I had to do ten more push-ups in ten seconds. My body shook and my fingers pulsated. I sweated profusely. I felt as if I were moving in slow motion, barely able to hear the time-keeper or the crowd.

"131,132, 133 . . . ," he shouted, his voice sounding far away. I continued to drop to the floor and touch my chest to the judge's hand to qualify for another push-up. I lifted my body slowly, arms shaking and beginning to spasm. The veins in my arms bulged; my leg muscles screamed, 'Stop!'

Faintly I heard, " . . . 138, 139, 140!" I had tied the world record in 75 seconds! With a second wind I shot out a burst of power and pumped fingertip push-up after fingertip push-up. "154!" the scorekeeper shouted. "TIME! 80 seconds!" I had done it! I had broken the Guinness world record! I was the new record holder in the Guinness World Book of Records doing 154 fingertip push-ups in 80 seconds! My friends crowded around congratulating me for putting another notch in my belt. I exulted in the thrill of victory.

Almost a year later I received a letter from Guinness congratulating me for having broken the existing record. However, the letter went on to say that, unfortunately for me, ten months later on July 2, 1978, Jim Ulrick had broken my record by doing 203 fingertip push-ups in 80 seconds. I was encouraged to try again.

Try again. Yeah, thanks—doing 203 fingertip push-ups in 80 seconds! Because I had not been the record-holder for 12 months, they regretted that my name would not be published in the World of Sports. Jim McKay's voice rang out, "The thrill of victory and the agony of defeat."

Las Vegas

With college and national competitions behind me, I still had a burning desire to push my body to its limits. I wanted more of that adrenaline rush. Glittering Las Vegas seemed as good a place as any to try out my acrobatic-jazz dancing talents. I had heard that the Tropicana Hotel had a show called the Folies Bergere; the pay was $450 per week. Sounded interesting to me!

Rob, a friend from Hinsdale, went with me to Las Vegas. We said our goodbyes and drove 250 miles to Iowa. Suddenly my 1975 Dodge Caravan made loud, pinging noises followed by a big bang. The engine smoked like a volcano. I could not believe that my brand-new van had let me down! It was 12:30 in the morning and we were exhausted. Rob and I managed to open the sizzling engine cover. Rob pulled the dipstick out. It was dry.

It was now 1 a.m. and very cold. Fortunately, we were stuck alongside Interstate 80 near an open gas station. The van was towed and the mechanic later told me that several rods and pistons had snapped in two and that the engine block had cracked. It would take him two weeks to order parts and repair the van. He slowly said, "Looking at the book parts . . . love to get you another engine. Maybe we can find one in the back." I vehemently refused saying that the engine was brand-new. "Was," he told me. "It's worthless now."

I told the man to hold off putting in the engine until he could order another one from the factory. I lied, telling him that the engine was faulty and that I didn't know why it had broken. Rob and I filled the engine with oil to cover my mistake. For the next two weeks we camped out at a nearby KOA campground. It was like seeing the movie Back to the Future. Everybody looked like they were from the 50's; the cars were antiques, Coke was five cents, and the people talked country. Boy, did I feel out of place! This was worse than Terre Haute.

Finally, we made it to Las Vegas. I had $200 left and Rob had $150. It did not matter; we were here! We gambled, got drunk, and slept in the van. After two weeks, Rob decided that this life was not so much fun and decided to take a bus home.

The Tropicana Hotel kept postponing my dance audition. I

called again and again. Finally after two weeks, the manager called me in. He liked what he saw and hired me as a substitute dancer. There was not much room on either side of the stage. Props like a full-sized Rolls Royce shared the cramped space with dancers stretching their legs and practicing their moves. Every night I waited behind the curtain as the six-foot, glittering ladies walked onto the gigantic stage and the acrobatic dancers flipped from side to side. I waited for someone to get hurt or take a vacation but no one ever did.

Life behind the curtain was not the same as life in front of it. The men were gay and the ladies were lesbians. The performers all swore and snorted cocaine. After the show they sat in front of large mirrors wiping off their make-up and talking about the parties they were going to that night. Without make-up these people were a sad sight.

Deciding that this was not what I wanted to do, I searched for another job. I scanned newspaper ads and called gyms with no success. At night I walked the streets for handouts, stole money from cars, jumped in at the primetime meal sites and looked for quarters in slot machines. I slept in my van, ate canned pork-and-beans and wore the same dirty clothes for days on end.

Finally I landed a minimum-wage job teaching gymnastics to preschoolers at a daycare center five hours a week. At a gym I found another weekly five-hour, minimum-wage job teaching high school kids gymnastics. I was making $150 a month and starving. I grew ill sleeping in my van, eating little and using public restrooms. If I didn't find an apartment soon, I was afraid I would need to be hospitalized.

I rented a room for $100 a month in a house full of prostitutes. Three of them had a combined weight of over 900 pounds! I didn't want any of their business, thank you very much. Fortunately, they did not work out of the home. They kept their distance and I kept mine. I slept on the sofa of a large woman with uncombed hair and tattoos—not a common sight in 1976. Her husband was a maximum-security prisoner.

She regularly came home around three in the morning. One night she had just come back from having had a huge fight with her husband. She swore and threw objects right at my head. I was afraid she might kill me. After almost six months of living like this, I felt so depressed that I decided to go to church. That Sunday I heard the preacher say that God loves me unconditionally. I recommitted my life to

Christ. Hope came back into my spirit and I gained a new perspective.

I found work teaching a couple of gym classes at a community center. I made it through to December when I told the gym administrator that I planned to quit. At the animal shelter I picked up a German shepherd-husky puppy as a Christmas gift for my parents. The little puppy and I drove towards home through the snowy Colorado mountains. Suddenly my van slid off the road and flipped over. My belongings and the puppy were tossed around inside the van. After everything settled, I heard the puppy yelp. I was relieved and thankful that he was in the back of the van, unhurt.

The van was upside down lodged at the bottom of a ravine. I could barely see through the snow-covered windshield. I struggled for minutes to open the passenger door, afraid that the engine would blow and catch fire. It was 10:30 at night and I could see nothing. The dimly lit highway above showed no sign of cars or trucks. Snow had filled the engine. I was scared. I struggled to open the windows but I was trapped. The temperature was minus 10°. My toes and fingers began to lose feeling.

"Oh, God, please help me," I prayed. "I feel like my life is in such a wreck. Please get me out of here!" Less than 10 minutes later a tow truck spotted me. A large man broke the door handle and pulled the dog and me out. The van was inoperable and had to be towed over 12,330 feet up the mountain to the nearest service station in Eagle, Colorado. Of course, at 1:00 a.m. no one was there.

In spite of the late hour, a mechanic miraculously showed up. I ran back down to the station in tears and told him my predicament. He wedged open the snow-filled engine. "The engine will have to be cleaned out," he said, "and the bill could be upwards of $200. Plus, it would take a couple days to fix."

The wind howled down the snow-covered street. I stuffed the puppy deep inside my jacket and trudged off, trusting that nobody would break into my van and steal my meager belongings.

I only had $150 and I needed a room. I couldn't afford to do both. In faith, I told the mechanic to go ahead and begin the repairs in the morning. It was now 1:30 a.m. on Christmas Eve. I had to find a place to stay. The poor little dog wouldn't stop whimpering. I searched all over town but there were no vacancies. My wet clothes had frozen and I couldn't feel my toes or fingers. Perspiration froze on my face. I had to find a place to sleep.

In spite of the No Vacancy sign in front of a motel, I banged on the office door. "We don't have any rooms," the manager grumbled. "Can't you read the sign?" He then told me to wait a minute and shut the door. I waited and waited. I feared my toes were frostbitten. The door finally opened and, much to my relief, the manager said I could stay in a room across the street. When I asked him how much it would cost, he brusquely said, "No charge." He gave me the key and told me to "Git." I couldn't believe it! I was shocked. Tears rolled down my cheeks and froze on my face. The little puppy was squirming and whimpering. Miraculously, the manager hadn't heard him. "Hey, we've got a room, little one! Thank you, God," I cried, "for taking care of me." I turned the key and stepped in. I turned on the shower and steamed up the bathroom. "Aaahh!" I exclaimed. The little puppy was seconding the relief. I turned the thermostat to 80° and pulled up a blanket to watch a *Johnny Carson* re-run. Feeling began to return to my toes and fingers. I thought everything was okay until I discovered that the puppy had peed all over the other bed. I felt so guilty!

It was 4:30 a.m. when I quietly slipped out of the motel with the puppy. I wandered the streets and then waited for the service station to open. By the grace of God the mechanic had arrived early and the little dog and I could wait inside the warm service station. My van would be fixed by noon. The bill was $100. Tired of living at the poverty level, I reluctantly called my parents. With only $50 left, I decided to drive back to Las Vegas and fly home to Chicago. Glad to hear from me, Mom and Dad graciously wired money for an airplane ticket. I didn't tell them where I had been living, that I wasn't working at the Tropicana, or that I was desperate for money.

I left the van in the airport parking lot, flew to Chicago and caught a bus home to Hinsdale. "Everything is going to be fine," I said to the little puppy whimpering in the crate. However, everything was not fine. My parents didn't want a dog for Christmas! They just couldn't handle a puppy at that time in their lives. I was shocked and saddened that my little furry friend would go to another pound. To my relief, later that week I learned that he had been adopted.

Christmas went by fast. I recuperated by relaxing, eating tons of food and getting back on the still rings. It was good to have my normal life back! At the gym I met Pete Yost, another gymnast who was with a Christian group called Athletes in Action. He invited me to come out to California and join the team. I would share my testimony at various college sites and teach kids gymnastics in the afternoon. It sounded great! I knew better times were ahead. I'd be making solid money and be around Christian gymnasts who loved the Lord!

In the interim, I flew back to Sin City. Walking to airport Parking Lot Seven, I saw my van. It was not as I had left it; it had been totally vandalized! The windows had been knocked out and the CB, TV and radio stolen. I couldn't believe it! I was speechless at what the thieves had done. I wanted to wring their necks! That was the final straw; I cleaned up the mess, put the gearshift into drive and never looked back . . .

. . . I slowly opened my eyes to see two familiar faces—my parents! "Dad! Mom! It's so wonderful to see you!" I greeted them with a big smile. We looked at each other lovingly for what seemed like hours. Dad came around to one side of my bed and nervously clutched my arm. Mom was on the other side. They simply held me and we cried.

"All I could think of was seeing you lying there," Dad nervously recalled. "I immediately left work in a stupor. When I got home your mother looked pretty shaken up from the news. We just held each other in the kitchen crying and not saying a word. Then I began to ask myself questions about what caused the accident. Was the equipment faulty? I wondered if you were covered by insurance and what would happen with nursing care." Because of Uncle Glenn, Dad knew all too well the practical side of a disability.

Dad walked to the window. "There was one good thing that happened. Last night I dreamt about Christ." I listened very carefully because my dad was not one to discuss his dreams. "Christ said in a voice kind and soft that he had seen our tears. He told me, 'I understand your concern but don't worry. All things are under control.'"

Dad looked at me, "God loves you and so do I!" Hearing my dad speak of Christ's love for me was like a cool drink in the hot desert. I knew that this dream was a special, God-given one. I knew because I had had the exact same dream that very same night!

❧ **Part 3: Strength in Weakness** ☙

Devastating Diagnosis

The next day I awoke to an attractive nurse who said she was taking care of me during the morning shift. If I needed anything I was to lean my head onto a buzzer pad right next to my head. I still could not take in that I had exchanged my once-vital body for one that might as well be on a slab in the morgue! I tried to calm down. Pray. Anything.

A few minutes later my surgeon, Dr. Bonnett, introduced himself in a baritone voice. After checking my vital signs he announced, "Well, Jack, I have good news and I have bad news. The good news is that you have feeling above the chest. The bad news is that you have no feeling or movement below." I stared at the doctor in shock and disbelief. My world was shattered by those five words--no feeling or movement below. I would never be on the rings again. I would never walk again. I would never use the restroom by myself ever again.

Life as I had known it was over. I would probably live out my days in a wheelchair—something I had never encountered as a young child. Although my youth group had caroled the invisible shut-ins behind curtains at Christmastime, everyone I knew looked perfect. That is, until I met my disabled Uncle Glenn for the first time when I was nine years old. He was my dad's older brother and because institutionalizing Glenn was out of the question, he lived with my grandparents in Clearwater, Florida.

As a young boy I used to wonder a lot about what Glenn might be thinking. Once he had been a strong, handsome young man. Growing up he and his brother Frank, my father, would wrestle on the living room floor after dinner. Uncle Glenn would always win. However, in his late teens Glenn suffered a brain aneurysm. Was he ever angry with God? Did he wish he could do things on his own? Did he ever feel left out of taking a girl out on a date, getting married or having children? He could not walk. He could not get out of bed without assistance or even cut up his meat. I had always felt uncomfortable around my uncle, afraid that I would become like him. Now my worst fears had become a reality. I lay there depressed beyond measure. Time ticked by minute after minute, hour after hour. Life as I had always lived it was over. 'The harder the challenge, the better' had always been my motto. Would I be able to live up to it now that I was faced with the hardest challenge I could possibly imagine?

Rehabilitation Institute of Chicago

After six weeks I was transferred from the Fountain Valley Medical Hospital intensive care unit to the Rehabilitation Institute of Chicago. The R.I.C. was world–renowned for providing the best care for the disabled. The 20-story Institute was a city in itself. Four floors were devoted to some 400 people with all sorts of disabilities. Four more floors were devoted to research design for devices like neck braces made out of lightweight alloys and wheelchairs fitted with the newest in everything. Other floors housed occupational and physical therapy, office space and food services.

The four-hour flight from California to Chicago was almost over. I was glad because my customized neck brace pinched. We circled Meigs Field overlooking Chicago, the Windy City. Mom looked with relief out the small port window to catch a glimpse of the lakefront. The Lear jet's engines shut off and as the hatch opened, I saw my sister Jeanne, her husband Ken and my brother Doug. Their faces registered dismay and compassion. The last time they had seen me, I was walking. Now that was a mere memory. The crew carefully moved me onto the waiting stretcher. An ambulance took Mom and me to the Institute as Dad drove behind with Ken, Jeanne and Doug.

As the ambulance pulled up to the front doors, I knew a chapter of my life had closed. I was no longer a gymnast but a member of the disabled community. That realization was quite emotional. Life seemed so unfair. Men and women relegated to wheelchairs had once lived active lives. Now because of an accident or disease they found them-selves in a completely different place. Their faces reflected heartache and loss—financial, physical, social and spiritual. Few smiled. Families, spouses and friends had deserted some of them because of denial and hopelessness. To me the disabled were lepers--outcasts, the forgotten. I began to ponder if I was like that. Would I lose hope? Would I become forever bitter at God?

A nurse wheeled me into the x-ray room to make sure my neck was stable after the long trip. From there I was rolled into an elevator and up to the seventh floor. In spite of being expected, I had to wait twenty minutes at the front desk until Jan, my nurse during the day shift, introduced herself. "Five foot two, eyes of blue," I thought to myself. "Is she a knockout! Things are looking up now! I thought they only had good-looking nurses in California!"

Jan rolled me down the long yellow and orange corridor to room 141. Four large hospital beds lined the wall; mine was next to the window. Jan then showed me the 'accommodations'—a roll-in shower, accessible closets, shelves and the toilet area. "If you need any help, this button will be right next to your head."

Two men who looked like bar bouncers transferred my weak body onto clean, white sheets. I almost fainted from the little movement. Turning my head I saw the Sears Tower and the John Hancock looming overhead. Cessna planes flew in the distance. Life on the outside seemed far away.

Mom and Dad unloaded my suitcase and stuffed animals friends had given me. They pinned get-well cards onto the corkboard behind me. The patient in the bed next to me was 22-year-old Stan who had been left a paraplegic by a car wreck. He had been in rehab for six months. To Stan's right was Brian, also injured in a car accident and completely paralyzed. Before entering rehab, he had spent 3 months in intensive care.

For the duration of my six-week stay at Fountain Valley Hospital, I had received Demerol injections in my arms and legs every four hours to reduce anxiety and pain. At R. I. C. I immediately entered a drug rehabilitation program. During withdrawals my temperature reached 103 degrees and my body shook painfully. I screamed for relief. Nurses supervised me around the clock to prevent shock.

I needed a fix. I tried to snap my neck by shaking my head. I wanted to die. A nurse placed her hands forcefully on my head to prevent further neck damage. She told my distraught parents that they would just have to wait it out. The hours dragged on as my sister Jeanne placed wet towels on my forehead while her husband Ken read Scriptures. Although I had been told that my injury would prevent me from sweating, I sure was proving them wrong! Twice a day my sheets were wringing wet. My speech was incoherent. Even though many people were praying for me, my body was fighting a battle.

On day seven, the shaking stopped. I could converse coherently and see clearly. With a lucid mind, I was riddled with guilt. I had been taught that a Christian was not depressed or angry. To compound my guilt, dozens of letters poured in from Christ Church of Oak Brook where my family attended. Athletes in Action, Moody Bible Institute and radio station WMBI listeners sent hundreds of get-well letters. I just could not open them. I felt like a hypocrite.

Fortunately, I did not have much time to dwell on spiritual matters. My daily schedule began at 7:30 a.m. with a strict regimen of suctioning my lungs, breathing treatments and a morning wash-down followed by range-of-motion exercises. Breakfast-in-bed was served at 9:00 followed by a generous serving of 20 pills. I had check-ups to be sure I did not have pressure sores. After a much-deserved lunch hour, the afternoon regimen consisted of more range-of-motion exercises, independent living skills and counseling followed by suctioning and breathing treatments. I had an hour of free time before dinner. How wonderful! My mind and body were worn out; the workouts rivaled gymnastics practices.

Thirty minutes' visitation followed dinner at 5:00 after which the night routine consisted of bladder and bowel care followed by bedtime preparation. A nurse placed headphones on my oversensitive ears, administered two Valiums for spasticity and positioned my head, back, and legs to prevent pressure sores. After catheterization, arm splints were placed on my wrists to keep them from dangling. Finally, velcro-strapped egg crate shoes were positioned to hold my feet at right angles. All that took one and a half hours. I felt like I was back under the tyranny of my gymnastics coaches, prepping us for an upcoming competition.

Because I often fainted attempting to sit up in bed, the next goal was to get me into a big, blue wheelchair. I was afraid to try it but the nurse left it next to my bed in case I changed my mind. All night I stared at the wheelchair silhouetted against the hall light. It symbolized fear, weakness, and dependence. I was not so sure I wanted to deal with that. "God, please help me. I'm scared," I whispered.

Morning light peeked through the curtains. My fear was tempered with hope, an expectancy that everything would be all right. I told the nurse I wanted to try sitting in the wheelchair. Two brawny men drew back the sheets and lifted me into the waiting chair. I closed my eyes. When I opened them, I was a little dizzy but excited. I felt like I was sitting in a dragster. The wheelchair was not so bad after all.

Nevertheless, as I talked about my fears associated with the wheelchair, I broke out in a cold sweat. My eyes rolled back in my head and I had to be transferred to my bed. In spite of that—through God's grace—I had met the challenge. That evening I shared my success story with my parents who were proud of me. We were all experiencing the 'new normal.'

I liked that my day attendant, Chuck, talked to me like a regular guy. "All right, Jack, wake up! It's time to get your carcass out of bed. I'm going to help you today so you better be a good boy, okay?" I loved his sarcastic banter. He never treated me like a 'sickie.' Sometimes he even cut my hair. It felt so good to be in style. Dragging my lifeless body out of bed and preparing for therapy was a chore. It took an hour and a half for Chuck to bathe and dress me before physical therapy.

I began to experience positive changes. Small things made a big impact. Sitting up at 60 degrees and moving my hand off the bed made the day worthwhile. After six weeks I had mastered sitting in the manual chair and was ready to try an electric Everest Jennings with blue leather. It looked like a Ferrari. Its aluminum glistened under the fluorescent lights. After showing me all the 'options,' my physical therapist, Bob, transferred me into the chair and snapped on the seatbelt. It felt great. After promising to go slow, I zoomed right into the wall! "I didn't realize it was so fast!" I sheepishly said. "I don't think I have enough strength in my shoulder to turn the control knob." Bob said that he would work with me on forearm exercises before I could try that 'Ferrari' again.

My goal was to build up strength to use the electric chair that promised independence. Up to this point, I had depended on someone to push me. I must have been on the 'armed and dangerous' list, but eventually I was able to go forward and turn without running into anything. I could keep up with my roommates in their fast, lightweight manual wheelchairs. I also could hold things in my lap. I even had the nurse open some of those encouraging letters I had been avoiding.

One morning a man I did not recognized stopped by. He introduced himself as Sam, one of the custodians. He had heard on his transistor radio that an All-American gymnast who had broken his neck was in rehab. Sam continued, "I thought that it must be you since I saw a picture of a gymnast above the bed. Your story really touched me and

I felt impressed to come over and pray for you." I told him that I would be honored as my tears welled up. After he prayed, Sam tipped his dusty hat and left. I never saw him again.

The next day I met Maggie, a physical therapist assigned to lead group exercises. During an hour-long session, she called out the commands as my parents gave their assistance. "All right, helpers," she ordered, "stretch your partner's legs sideways, up and down. Again: one, two, three. Stretch the legs sideways, up and down."

I love challenges—the harder, the better. It is what I live for! I held my leg for five seconds then nearly fainted! We repeated this five times. Next, Mom lifted my elbow and wrist at 90° and helped me 'jab the sky.' We jabbed the sky 50 times. Then I raised the other arm 50 times. Lifting my arm felt like I was lifting my full body weight.

After a couple of months I graduated from one-pound weights to two-pound weights. Mike, another physical therapist, was very impressed with my determination. He helped me out on the slings, a contraption used to hook up my arms and legs so that they could move easier. For the first time, I used my triceps, an unheard-of feat for a quadriplegic. The doctors had told me that I would never move my wrists, let alone my triceps!

As the months rolled by, my triceps began to support my body weight as I got in and out of my electric wheelchair. Meanwhile, in occupational therapy Ruth worked with me using a VIF scale, a weird-looking mechanism that balanced my arm so I could move my hands. My job was to separate shaped blocks into their boxes, to type and to learn independent living skills. It was wonderful to regain some independence. Each day I felt stronger and more thankful.

Every Tuesday I took a one-hour drawing class. At first I was discouraged because I could not move my arm, much less draw. Before my accident I was able to draw with ease for hours. From the age of seven I had enjoyed drawing. When I was in grade school Mom would take me down to the Art Institute of Chicago. Portraits jumped out from the canvas as if the person were alive. I wondered what the subjects might have been thinking. I marveled at Van Gogh's Starry Night, Rembrandt's portraits and Monet's impressionistic works. I felt like a kid in a candy store. After the field trip I would go to my room and take out my sketchbook and try to copy them. I loved the challenge of discovering how each painter drew and used colors. The more I studied the paintings, the more I saw and marveled at the God-given talent of these artists.

It seemed that I, too, had a God-given gift for accurately drawing figures and objects. I spent hours enjoying one thing I could do without struggling. I drew bowls, boxes and apples. I studied shapes at different angles--straight on, overhead, close-up and from a distance. Then I gradually used hand-eye coordination to let the pencil direct the emerging shape on paper. Leonardo da Vinci's Last Supper and self-portraits along with Michelangelo's paintings in the Sistine Chapel sparked my enthusiasm for copying da Vinci's work. Many times I felt inadequate to the task but as time progressed I gained confidence. With each art book I studied and each class I took I learned more about perspective, shading, shadowing and color.

Now, although my fingers were not directly grabbing onto the pencil, I made tremendous progress. My arm slowly moved across the paper making large, squiggly lines. Then I tried to write my initials "J. F." in a 5" x 5" box. The pencil ran off the table. I felt depressed about having to start all over again. On so many levels I had to start all over again. I felt like a baby with an adult's mind.

Later, when I met Joni Erickson again after my accident and saw her paintings, I was awestruck. I said to myself that if Joni can paint with a brush in her mouth, I can paint with the limited grip of my hands. I knew this would be a way to regain some of my past talent in art.

I began to gain more understanding of how God was working in all this. Ironically, I had wanted to be free from the chair when in reality the chair was the very springboard which helped break down the barriers. However, many challenges remained.

My temperature often shot up to 100.3°. My eyes became bloodshot and sweat rolled off my forehead. I drifted in and out of consciousness. Within thirty minutes I was unable to control my breathing. My clothes were ripped off and ice packs were placed on all my arteries. They felt cold but they did the job! Within two hours, the fever lowered to 100°.

My team of doctors gave their patients the opportunity to visit their families for a weekend during the holidays. Was I overjoyed! I looked forward to no wake-up calls, no nurses, no shots, no pills. The wind whipped off Lake Michigan and the temperature was 20 degrees as I waited to board the ambulance that would take me to Hinsdale, my childhood home. I was freezing! By the time the ambulance attendant boarded me, my body had spasmed into a surfboard. It took all his strength to bend my legs onto the footrests and wedge me into the van. Dr. Carle had warned me that my body would be out of control at times. My stiff legs left me nostalgic for the superhuman days when I was in control of my body. It very was depressing to realize that instead of being the master of my body, I had become subject to it.

As the ambulance drove to Hinsdale, I was vexed that things would not be the same at 621 W. Hickory. I could not relax in my own room because the medical bed would not fit. My 'room' was out in the living room where I had no privacy. Lying in a medical bed amidst a boatload of braces, tubes and leg bags felt strange. My hearing had become so super-sensitive that the noise of doors banging and dishes clanging was unbearable.

Christmas Day arrived and I felt unsure about how the whole morning would go. I did not want to be the center of attention and spoil the fun. Dad asked my brother, Doug, to be Santa. When he gave me my first gift I had to ask him to turn the card over to see who it was from and to open the gift. That was difficult for me because I had been so independent and self-sufficient. Even Doug was caught off guard because it was a new experience for him. The gift actually was from him. As he ripped it open, he said, "It's a book about whales and dolphins. I thought you would enjoy it since you were a scuba diver." Everyone was silent. Doug knew he had hit a nerve. I swallowed the memory as I tried to be upbeat as Doug flipped through the colorful pages.

Maintaining a positive attitude and not ruining Christmas Day for the whole family was a real battle. I struggled to hold back tears remembering how I used to build a snowman in the backyard, go ice skating down at Burns Field and walk on my hands down the hallway.

Monday came quickly and I was relieved I had to go back to rehab for more therapy. The weekend had gone relatively smoothly, but in reality I was grateful I didn't have to be in my house that carried so many good memories during such a hard time. Being completely paralyzed while watching my family tearing open presents and drinking hot chocolate was too much to bear.

It would take some time before I could authentically be glad to be in the presence of friends and loved ones who were laughing and enjoying themselves when there was now so much I could not do. The transition would take many, many months.

Now it was July 7, 1980. It had been nearly six months since I had been flown from California to recuperate at the Rehabilitation Institute of Chicago. Dr. Carle, head of the spinal cord unit, told me that I was ready to leave, but my parents were without attendants to help me at home. The insurance company said that they could get help for me within twenty-four hours through agencies. All this was confusing and frustrating.

Attendants were another challenge that seemed like a never ending list of duties. Nevertheless, my dad's plan of attack was to hire two attendants to take over the nurses' duties. Mom put ads in the newspapers and asked around to see if our friends knew of anyone—a college student or friend—who might like to help out. In the meantime, Dad and Mom would have to remember the techniques that they learned at the rehab. After two weeks of getting me up, feeding me, doing bladder and bowel care, and the nighttime routine, my parents showed signs of wear and tear. We argued about important and trivial things and I felt like God did not care about me.

Saying goodbye to my family was hard. They all had been part of healing the inner wounds of the trauma, yet my heart was to reconnect with my gym buddies back in California. The Athletes in Action team along with Tim Micklin and attendant Benny Plocich greeted me at the airport. We hugged as they said, "Welcome back, Jack. We've been praying for you."

I was anxious to start over and enjoy where I had left off and to become stronger and to be a part of the team. But as the weeks rolled by, I realized that my expectations of fitting in did not match with reality. I could not escape the fact that I was not the same person training to compete in the next gym meet. The team tried to include me as a coach but it was breaking my heart. Besides I did not want to instill fear in any of the gymnasts. Life had drastically changed and their attempt to include me was too painful.

One night as Benny helped me into bed, I thought of a letter from Joni. "Please let me know if yours is a permanent disability. Stay in touch." The next day I called her and we talked, prayed and cried. I became a part of her ministry team. I felt like I could encourage others who could use God's healing touch. I began to share my testimony with groups and individuals across the San Fernando Valley and then nationally. It fulfilled my need to feel useful. My parents were relieved that the transition—difficult as it was for them—was going well. I moved to Woodland Hills near Los Angeles where Joni's ministry, Joni and Friends, was located. Bob Jordan took over the attendant care responsibilities.

For two years I worked with Joni and Friends speaking on Joni's behalf around the country. In 1984 Joni asked me to represent her at First Presbyterian Church of Hollywood. Reverend Lloyd Ogilvy, wearing his traditional black robe, introduced me to the congregation of 1,500. An usher pushed me up the long ramp onto the stage and I shook Dr. Olgilvy's hand as I gazed out over the sanctuary.

I stuttered for a moment, speaking to a world-famous minister and author whom I had seen on TV and heard on the radio. I explained that Joni and Friends needed their support in welcoming the disabled to

Hollywood Pres. As I talked I realized that my leg bag had opened and was draining around our feet. Reverend Ogilvy didn't seem to notice and continued to ask me questions about Joni and Friends. Fortunately the stage was elevated and the congregation could not see the puddle. After ten minutes I did not know if anything I had said made sense. As Dr. Ogilvy thanked me for sharing, the audience clapped, oblivious to what occurred. I left the stage feeling humbled, wondering why God would allow such a thing to happen. Dr. Ogilvy never mentioned it.

Radio Ministry

I met Betty who hosted Ray of Hope, a radio ministry that presented Bible lessons for the disabled, at the Orange County Fair. I shared my testimony with her and the next week she invited me to speak on her half-hour radio show. I was petrified and excited as Betty introduced me to the manager of KYMS, who in turn introduced me to the board tech man who oversaw sound and levels. The station's range covered Orange County and Betty's show aired between Chuck Smith and Chuck Swindoll. I felt the pressure!

As Betty and I sat facing a solid glass wall, the soundman said over our headphones, "Ready? 5,4,3,2,1 - go."

"Today, I have a special guest . . ." and before I knew it the interview was over. Later that week Betty called to say that she had she had contracted scarlet fever and would not be able to continue hosting the program. When Betty said she was impressed with my story, I asked her if I could take over the show. Each week I was the man behind the microphone sharing Bible lessons with the listeners. Since the shows were recorded, I could hear myself on the radio while I was taking a shower. My voice sounded so 'Mickey-Mouse' compared to the heavy-weights. Ray of Hope lasted one year. How did that happen? It was a God-thing. To this day I don't know how I survived.

Meeting Maria

In 1980 I had my van modified. When I moved to Woodland Hills I stored it in Tim's garage and bought a BMW 320i sports car modified with hand controls. Getting out, I would transfer quickly to my wheelchair on the passenger side then pull the door shut. Ninety percent of the time the transfer did not work completely and I would ask somebody on the street to close the door. I was so stubborn! I had started going to the Valley Vineyard in Tarzana when I met Maria in the church parking lot. I was trying to pull my manual wheelchair into my sports car and the spokes were stuck on the door handle. Even after two years of family and friends telling me to get an accessible van, I still wouldn't listen. I maintained the gymnastics mentality of self-reliance. I tried every which way to get the wheel loose without success. Sweat poured off my forehead. Cursing under my breath and raging at God, I spewed anger at my unresponsive body. I demanded to be independent and do things by myself—and to get the chair into the passenger seat! Maria, who saw me struggling, approached me slowly and said, "Do you need some help?"

I said, "No! I don't need any help! Get out of here! I can do it myself!"

She took a step backward and said, "Oh, okay!"

Twenty minutes later everybody had left the parking lot except for her and me. Maria had been doing some cleanup work in her classroom when she came out and spotted me again. "I'm leaving now. Do you need some help?" I reluctantly accepted her offer. I hated asking for help. Maria was a very pretty girl and it had been many years since I had talked to a girl as pretty as she was. Generally people were uneasy with my being in a wheelchair. They didn't know what to say or how to help so I was surprised that Maria stuck around even after I had yelled at her. I thought about her willingness to help me during the following week. We saw each other in church the next week. I knew she was beginning to like me although I later learned that I still had some 'quirks' she was unsure about.

Two weeks later I was in the same predicament with the manual wheelchair stuck in the door handle. Maria again saw me struggling and losing my temper. She came around to my car's front door and introduced herself again. "Hi, I'm Maria, the person that helped you a few weeks ago. I see that you're struggling again. Do you need some help getting your chair in?"

I was about to tell her off and say no but I liked her cute face and body. I didn't want to push her away again, so reluctantly I accepted. When she asked if she could do anything else, I hesitated for a moment and then—with all the courage I could muster—I asked her out on a date even though a voice inside was screaming, "You're stupid. She won't like you. She's going to say, 'Sorry.'"

I was about to close the door, ignore the rejection and move on with my life when Maria smiled and said, "Yes, I'd love to!" I was stunned. I just sat there in complete shock. After salvation, this was the best thing that had happened in my life! As she walked away, I checked her out and was in awe. I later learned that as Maria walked to her car, she heard a voice whisper in her spirit saying, "You're looking at your future husband." She was taken aback but kept it in her heart.

As I drove away, my thoughts raced. Did Maria really want to date me? Surely, I couldn't tell her about my leg bag and all the things that were wrong with my body. That night I very nervously called her. We had a lot of things in common She liked going to the movies, she liked talking about deep things, and she had a funny laugh! Most of all, she loved the Lord! Maria didn't pity me; she really cared about who I was. She saw my perseverance plus I think she liked my sports car. The more we talked, the more I fell in love with her.

On one occasion Maria and I were driving to the beach and my leg bag was so full it was going to burst. I thought if she knew I needed to empty it, Maria would just want to go home but when I told her she said, "Fine, let's pull off the road and I'll help you!" Little did I know that her background was helping stroke patients in physical therapy. It was no big deal for Maria; for me, it was huge.

On our first date at Marie Callender's, Maria wore a pretty blue dress that matched her eyes. I was nervous but the evening was going well when Maria confronted me. "You know, I think you're a great guy but you joke all the time and put yourself down too much. You need to grow up and become more real!" I was shocked by her bluntness. Sitting at the table, I thought about it in utter silence. I wanted to just take her home. Besides I no longer wanted to pay for her meal! As the minutes ticked by, I knew Maria was right about my joking all the time to cover up my feelings. I was amazed that she was able to honestly say what she was thinking. I was even more amazed that she cared more about my character than my façade. As Maria talked I realized that my conversation had been all about me and what I had accomplished and all the awards I had won. Maria helped me see that what I needed to do was to think about the other guy rather than myself. When I often complained about the abilities that I had lost, Maria gave me permission to vent my anger. Nevertheless, she didn't allow me to think that being able to walk, run and jump would free me from my problems. Her goal was to help me move through these deep resentments.

Maria dating me was a big step for both of us. Were we to marry, she would have a huge responsibility caring for me. She'd also have to assume household chores that normally an able-bodied husband would assume such as washing the dishes, taking out the trash and fixing leaky faucets. My responsibility would be to care about her and to listen to what was in her heart and mind. One of the ways I chose to show Maria I cared was by writing a series of letters to her, even though we lived a mere ten miles apart. Through these letters, we found that our similarities outweighed the negatives. God was at the core of our relationship. As we worked together, we saw that I could help out in different ways.

At the time Maria was teaching fourth grade at a private school. She asked me if I would like to observe her. After school she told me I should consider teaching. "You've got the heart to care for children. I think you'd be a great teacher!"

During these months of dating Maria and observing her teaching, my care attendant Bob Piocich was there for me one hundred percent. As we talked late into the night, he calmed my fears about not being a good husband. He encouraged me to take the big step, to propose marriage. One evening I asked her if she would like to get married and she said, "Yes!" We called our parents and asked them what they thought. They were all for it! We went to the jeweler and had gold rings engraved with Song of Solomon 4:7 "You are altogether beautiful, my darling; there is no flaw in you."

During our engagement Maria helped me organize my life into morning, afternoon and evening routines. She explored our financial options. I was covered under Worker's Compensation and received monthly attendant care checks plus the policy covered all medical expenses. She advised me to sell the sports car and have my van customized with hand controls, a swivel seat for easy transfer to my wheelchair and a ramp to make it accessible. She also suggested that I order a scooter so that I would not have to work so hard with my wheelchair. I felt degraded by all these changes; I saw myself as more disabled than when I was driving my sports car.

Nevertheless, another major hurdle was over and we became closer as the months went by. We talked about our marriage but that seemed like a long way off as we discussed how she would take care of my needs such as getting into bed and having relations. In order to make ends meet, Maria said she would be my attendant. That she was going to hang in there and take care of me seemed very lopsided to me. However, my responsibility was to be the breadwinner by becoming a teacher. I had many doubts because I was disorganized. I was not confident about riding a scooter let alone controlling a class, but I told her I'd give it a try.

In preparation for our wedding, Maria gave me two things to do: (1) order tuxedos for my dad and brother Doug and (2) arrange the rehearsal dinner. She said she would do the rest. I was glad because I was never organized! I called Dad and Doug to get measurements for their tuxedos. I gave the information to the Sears tailor and had Dad and Doug fly out to be fitted two days before the wedding. When the three of us went for the fitting, the tailor brought out the two tuxedos and they tried them on. Doug's pants were dragging on the ground and Dad's pants were just past his knees. They looked like Laurel and Hardy! I felt horrible and embarrassed and Dad was not very happy. They were re-measured while I felt like hiding in a hole.

To arrange the rehearsal dinner, I called a local French restaurant and asked the manager if I could come down and choose a few items from their menu. The man on the phone spoke French and some broken English. When I arrived at the restaurant, I found that the menu was written entirely in French! Mom had said she wanted prime rib with baked potatoes and green beans. I pointed to the first selection thinking it was what I needed. The manager nodded his head, made a transaction and said, "Avoir, monsieur."

The night of the rehearsal dinner a hundred guests sat at round tables. Maria and I and the bridal party were seated on the stage. The maître d' and his five servers brought out the meals on covered, silver platters. They first served my mother and father. When they took the lids off the silver platters, what my mom saw was not prime rib but hamburger!

Angrily, Mom stood up, banging her fists on the table, "I did not order hamburger meat; I ordered prime rib!" Maria was as silent as the guests. She kicked me in the shin under the table and said in a harsh tone, "What did you do? You made me look like a fool! I gave you a couple things to do and you messed up!" She looked at me sternly, "Do something quickly!"

I was stunned. I had to think of something quick. I was praying like I'd never prayed when I got an idea. I summoned the maître d' to my table. "Do you happen to have a 50-pound, well-done prime rib in your oven?" With a heavy French accent he said, "I don't think so, but I'll check!" As he went back to the kitchen the five servers rolled out trashcans and one by one dumped the dinners. Maria tried to look like nothing had happened by turning away and talking to the bridal party. I felt alone and stupid.

Minutes later, the maître d' came back from the kitchen and said to me, "You know what, I looked in the oven and there actually is one, cooked well done!"

Ten minutes later the maître d' and his servers carried out new dinners on covered silver platters. Mom, who was served first, said, "Now, that's more like it!"

At three a.m. I called Maria to ask forgiveness for my stupidity. I asked her if she still wanted to marry me. She did not answer so I said, "Well, I'll see you in the morning at the church." She said nothing. The next morning my family and friends met at the church. It was one hour before the wedding and no sign of Maria. As the bridal party and I stood up on the stage, the music began 'Here comes the bride all dressed in white.' Maria came around the corner dressed in white, flowers cascading from her wrists. She was beautiful. I couldn't believe that she still cared for me. Our eyes locked and I felt like we were alone in the sanctuary. I felt like we were one and she was mine! I began to cry as she walked towards me with a radiant smile. Our families and friends were also crying. As Maria held my hand at the altar and we said our vows, I knew she cared for me and I deeply cared for her. With God's help we would make it.

After the ceremony, the music played and people clapped. Maria sat on my lap as I rolled down the aisle towards the door. The farther we went, the slower the scooter went. I looked up and saw that Maria's dress was caught under the right wheel. She motioned to me in fear that her dress was going to be pulled right off her body. I put the scooter in reverse. People turned around with bewildered looks wondering why we were going back to the altar. A gentleman saw what was happening and graciously removed Maria's dress from under the wheel. People clapped in relief as we rolled out the back doors.

After less than one day of marriage I knew it would be a challenge, but how much of one we would soon see. As part of our honeymoon we drove up the coast of California to Pebble Beach Country Club, a world-renowned, five-star resort. As I parked the car my bowels emptied. I could not believe that after a wonderful wedding such a horrible thing could happen to us. I cried as Maria consoled me, transferred me into the wheelchair and pushed me into the lobby. In the absence of a family bathroom we decided to use the men's room. After looking left and right, we made our way quickly into the bathroom and headed for the handicapped stall.

Unfortunately, it was too small to accommodate my wheelchair so Maria stripped me in front of the sink. As she was pulling off my clothes, a golfer walked in. Assaulted by the odor of excrement mixed with liquid soap, he took one quick look and made an even quicker exit. Maria and I looked at each other and said, "Oh, well, what can you do?"

Half an hour later we made our way out the door leaving behind wastebaskets overflowing with filthy paper towels. I felt humiliated and loaded down with despair because Maria had to persevere through the episode. Years later, we look back and laugh remembering how we survived that first trial.

Abigail

In 1994, after nine years being married, Maria conceived. We had a daughter. We chose the name Abigail. The day came and Abigail was born, a perfectly healthy baby girl. The love I had for Maria and Miss Ab. was without words.

On afternoon strolls, I carried her close to my heart in a pouch. When she turned two, Maria hooked a trailer hitch and carrier onto the back of my scooter. Up front, our basset hound Chumley was attached to the neck of the scooter. Neighbors would wave and smile whenever they saw the three of us roll by. As she got older Abigail would stand between my legs and hold onto the handlebar. Then she graduated to riding a tricycle and with Maria's help rode her bicycle alongside me.

Maria had many creative ways for me to participate actively in Abigail's childhood experiences. On Saturdays, Brittany, a mother's helper, and I would take Abigail to Gymboree, an indoor play gym. I encouraged Abigail as Brittany assisted her with tumbling. I enjoyed watching her climb the tubes, looking at me through the top one. Connecting with my daughter through smiles and waves brought joy to my heart. Afterwards we enjoyed chicken McNuggets. When Abigail was older, she even tried gymnastics, learning handstands and cartwheels.

Maria and I both wanted Abigail to be familiar with various sports so that she could participate with her friends. For several summers she took tennis lessons at Pierce College. Maria enrolled Abigail in volleyball leagues. I'd always root for her team and after the game we would either celebrate or commiserate with an ice cream or soda. I was proud of Abigail's talent and motivation.

Our family enjoyed ourselves in creative ways as well. After dinner the three of us would sing into the microphone pretending to perform onstage before an appreciative and applauding audience. Abigail loved playing Cossette in *Les Miserable*. At Christmastime I would invite family and friends to perform Charles Dickens' *A Christmas Carol* complete with costumes and sound effects. We all laughed as we acted out our parts.

Each summer the three of us drove to Forest Home for their father/daughter retreat. Maria graciously assisted me but stayed out of sight so I could spend time alone with Abigail. I was relieved that my daughter was not embarrassed about having the only dad in a wheelchair. Although I would have liked to participate in water sports, Abigail and I connected during the evenings in the art cabin painting wooden figures. Afterwards we would stroll down to the soda bar and order milkshakes. That was wonderful!

During Abigail's elementary and high school years, Maria and I always attended Open House to view her schoolwork. Some mornings I would drive 'Miss Ab' to high school. On the way we listened to Chuck Swindoll on the van's radio. At the end of the program Abigail and I would recite the address and telephone number in unison.

Growing up, Abigail had watched as Maria prepared me for work, helped me around the house and performed my bedtime routines. I feel sure that inspired Abigail to volunteer as a candy striper at Valley Presbyterian Hospital during her junior and senior years of high school. She always had some funny stories to share with us about her shift. Maria would drop her off at four o'clock in the afternoon and I would pick her up at eight in the evening. Seeing my little girl dressed in her red scrubs brought tears to my eyes.

We felt proud when Abigail's senior class elected her Class President. Dropping her off for Prom was hard. My heart felt heavy seeing her all dressed up and waving goodbye as she went to meet her friends. I could barely see through my tears. I realized that the years I had spent with her were drawing to a close. When Abigail left home for college, I knew that she had grown up. I am very grateful that we thought of many opportunities for me to be included in Abigail's memories.

Scuba Diving

Growing up in landlocked—and often chilly—Illinois, I often remembered the warm, clear Florida seawater. I spent Saturday nights watching Jacques Cousteau explore reefs, sea life and caves on PBS. That is what inspired me to learn scuba diving. My memories drifted back to when I was a student at Indiana State University where I learned diving basics in an Olympic-sized pool. I then enrolled in an advanced course. I will never forget the final exam—a night dive in a quarry, the muddy bottom littered with sleeping perch and lake worms. Not exactly a Jacques Cousteau experience, but I was determined to return to the Gulf of Mexico.

After passing the course I saw an advertisement in a diving magazine for a live-aboard charter boat to the Bahamas departing from Islamorada, Florida for one week. I had saved up my money from cutting lawns and selling seeds, and my parents reluctantly said I could go. I was so pumped up! Nothing scared me—that is until I saw the movie *Jaws*. I had nightmares of 25-foot great white sharks lurking below the Gulf's surface. Nevertheless, I drummed up my courage and flew to Key West and took a bus to Islamorada.

The first night a violent storm tossed the ship up the crest of a wave and then straight down 30 feet as the captain frantically called the Coast Guard. The twenty of us divers and crew were thrown every which way—like a soggy load of old socks cycling through a clothes dryer. Most of us tossed our cookies that night—and I don't mean the kind young girls bring to our doors each Spring. It was an evening of upheaval that nobody slept through and none of us likely ever forgot.

The next morning we all lay dazed and exhausted on the deck. If this was the first day, what was the next week going to be like? I wanted to go home. That morning I saw no sign of huge waves, only swirls resembling a toilet bowl flushing. The captain nonchalantly explained that blue and black holes created by volcanoes—some 5,000 feet deep—had a suctioning effect on aircraft and ships. We were in the Bermuda Triangle! We all fearfully remembered stories of ships and airplanes being sucked into the vortex, never to be seen again.

I knew one thing: I was not going into that dangerous water, no-sir-ee. No sooner had I made this vow than the ship's cigar-chomping captain barked at me gruffly, "Buddy, you've come this far and you're not going to stay on this boat." With that he nonchalantly pushed me over the edge into the unforgiving sea.

As I began to swim away from the ship, I felt the stings of hundreds of tiny jellyfish. The bloom extended down three feet. Not more than one minute later a three-foot silverfish mackerel exposed three rows of teeth as it swam up to my mask. The regulator popped out of my mouth as I gulped salt water. The large mackerel then proceeded through a large school of Jackfish, slicing them to pieces. As the remains sank to the bottom, the large fish scooped them up into his mouth.

During that week my partner Bill and I saw tiny turtles zigzag across the sand of a deserted island. We dove into the black swirls to find debris sucked in by the Bermuda Triangle. Diving into that danger-ous area, I felt like a government official searching for missing ships. We came upon a 150-foot-long World War II destroyer wedged between the walls of coral. We also located an airplane in shallow waters caught in the reef. On our last day Bill and I dove 30 feet and came upon a colony of large conches. Picking one off the sandy bottom actually was a Jacque Cousteau moment.

After I broke my neck, I thought my days of scuba diving were over, but my zeal for diving had not waned. Every time I looked at my gear I cried. One day I swallowed my pride and looked in the Yellow Pages under 'Scuba Diving for the Disabled.' To my surprise Don and Laura Hutchinson from Ontario, California, were part of the Hand-icapped Scuba Association (HAS) and certified to teach the blind or paralyzed--folks like me! I called and told them I used to dive. "Great!" Don exclaimed. "We'd love to train you." I drove out to their home, watched videos, read the manual, took the test and after three months, passed the course.

The first time they squeezed my old gear on it seemed like it was not going to work. After being paralyzed for five years my legs and arms had atrophied leaving my wetsuit oversized. Once again, I was sadly reminded that I was no longer in control of my body. Having little movement below my neck made getting into the water a scary propo-sition, but with the encouragement of my two instructors I learned to breathe underwater with a tank.

Next they got me in touch with Denise Dowd, an advanced ocean instructor with HSA. She trained me using underwater hand signals, buddy breathing in case one of our tanks failed and balancing as she propelled me through the water. I trained in a Santa Barbara pool for many months on Saturday afternoons. Denise and Robert, another HSA instructor, fitted me with a new wetsuit, tank, breathing apparatus, boots, and regulator.

After six months we were ready. At Two Rivers, Catalina, off the coast of Los Angeles, we boarded a dive boat and headed through the dark green waters to the dive site. Robert and Denise lay me on my back on the deck to make putting on my wetsuit easier. Robert pulled the wetsuit up over my knees. Denise made sure my catheter and leg bag were secure.

By the time they pulled the wetsuit up over my hips to my chest, I was hot from lying in the sun. "I am getting faint," I told Denise. "Quadriplegics don't sweat." She nodded and gave me a large glass of water. I began to feel better and my head stopped pounding. Robert sat me up and held me from behind as Denise pulled the wetsuit arms on and zipped up the top.

The boat made its way around the cove to the backside of Catalina where the waves were calmer. As we stopped 100 yards off the rocks, a deckhand unleashed the rope and tossed the dark gray anchor into the waters. I began to feel a nervous reservation about this 'adventure.' By now all of the other divers had checked their regulators, making sure the tanks was delivering oxygen and jumped in. I gave a thumbs-up as Robert and Denise slid me off the deck and onto the stair. I could not believe I was doing this. It had been 25 years since I had put my feet into the ocean.

My mask felt claustrophobic at first but after my tank and straps were centered on my back, Denise grabbed me under my arms and slowly slipped me into the murky water. I gasped as the 60-degree water made its way through my wetsuit. Denise assured me that it would take a few minutes to regulate my body heat. For a brief moment I mistakenly thought I could swim and balance upright by moving my arms. The truth was that I was paralyzed and fully dependent on my instructors.

As the waves rolled over my face, I took in a mouthful of seawater. Choking, gasping for air and continuously coughing, I feared that

I was going to drown, but Denise kept me upright. Nevertheless, I was afraid not only that I was swallowing too much water, but that—remembering the movie Jaws—a big shark was going to attack me! As I tried to remain calm, I could faintly hear a man on board asking if I was all right.

I was only two feet under the surface when I panicked and spit out the regulator. Denise immediately grabbed my shoulder and pulled me to the surface. I felt anxious from taking in too much seawater and being unable to see far in the murky water. Balancing in the water as a quadriplegic was far more challenging than I had ever imagined. Nevertheless, after coming this far I was determined to succeed.

As Denise swam alongside me, we encountered fish—large and small—darting through a 50-foot swaying kelp. I seemed to be in a giant aquarium. I could not believe that I had recaptured a moment from the past, a moment that I had thought was gone forever.

When the underwater current threatened to tangle us in seaweed, Rob swam ahead parting the kelp. Suddenly a five-foot sea lion shot out of nowhere and stuck its nose in front of my mask. I was amazed at how graceful and beautiful she was as she turned and darted away in the dark water.

Fifty feet below the boat we started to ascend stopping every five feet for one minute to prevent the bends. When we reached the bobbing waves, I smiled at Rob and Denise with relief. I could still scuba dive! The crew shouted happily as a strong man grabbed under my arms and lifted me out of the water. Denise and Rob quickly got my wetsuit off, dried me and put warm clothes on me. I was in awe that God had helped me to fulfill a dream and that with Denise and Rob's help, I had regained a lost joy.

Once Denise invited the mayor of Catalina to dive with us. He was as curious as the other divers about how a quadriplegic could be a part of the experience. We all slipped below the ocean's surface and marveled at the beauty of God's creation. Later, as we ascended, I was surprised to see an ambulance on the dock and two paramedics waiting at the stairway. Many divers and onlookers were concerned that I had gotten the bends and had called for help, but the mayor called back to them that the diver was a quadriplegic and that he was just fine.

On another occasion, off Anacapa Island, our goal was to cave dive and land inside a room. I hung onto Denise's arm as the underwater current swooshed us into a cave opening. Rob and Denise did not have to assist me in kicking my fins as we made our way through the rocky crevice and down the hallway to the cave room. Within seconds we had removed our masks and loud echoes of crashing waves and our voices bounced off the walls. We put our masks back on and dove, exiting the cave. Within seconds the current, like a giant hand, pushed us out into the open sea. Looking back we saw lobsters, Garibaldi fish and eels around the cave's entrance. My heart raced with ecstatic joy. My friends had helped me to experience what cave diving was all about. That night I could not sleep thinking about the privilege my friends had given me.

I felt relaxed in the water, but during one of our dives my regulator popped out of my mouth and flew back onto my tank. As I lay on the ocean floor for what seemed like minutes, Rob and Denise desperately shared their regulators so I could take a few breaths. I closed my eyes thinking each one might be my last. When Denise brought around my regulator and stuck it in my mouth, I began to breathe easier. I motioned for us to return to the boat. We swam over to the anchor and slowly made our way up the chain to the surface. That was the last time I went scuba diving. The waters were too cold and I felt my time was up. Nevertheless, ten more years of diving had stored up a lot of good memories!

Sledding

In addition to scuba diving, I briefly participated in another sport. I heard about sledding for the disabled from my friend Bob who wore leg braces because of having had polio. On the Internet I saw pictures of disabled people sitting in a sled with a ski instructor holding onto the back.

I contacted an instructor who assured me that I was going to have a great time because he would make sure I would be safe while creating a positive, lasting memory. The plan was for my friend, Jim, to ski backwards in front of the sled and for another friend, Terry, to tie a towrope around the back of the sled to slow me down as we descended. Jim started pulling the sled as he skied backwards down the hill. Terry pulled back securely on the towrope as I guided the poles. Within seconds the sled picked up speed. Snowflakes and ice collected on my mask, restricting my vision, but wiping it off while holding onto the poles was impossible. Even though I had limited use of my arms, some maneuvers were clearly out of my range. Jim showed strain from skiing backwards and then *BOOM*! He hit an oncoming skier, sending him into a mound of snow.

Terry pulled his skis together in a snowplowing effort to slow down the 'bullet.' Yanking on the towrope, he leaned back as the sled picked up speed, taking out oncoming skiers. He told me to lean over and dig my poles hard into the snow. I tried but the hard-packed snow grabbed them out of my hands. I closed my eyes as my leg bag exploded and freezing pee crusted my lower body. I leaned hard to the left and the sled spun in three circles, coming to rest upside down. That was my first and last sledding experience. So much for another 'The harder the challenge, the better!'

Teaching Years

I enrolled in the Education Department at California State University, Northridge. The supervisor bluntly told me that in the last 60 years no quadriplegic teacher had gone through the program. I did not know what to say but I was willing to give it a try. Reluctantly, he signed me up. Besides being physically disabled, I had another hurdle to overcome: I was also learning disabled. Dyslexia had prevented me from attaining grades higher than a C in the past. CSUN required B's to fulfill the graduation requirements. I would need a tutor and would have to study twice as hard. The tutor would take notes in class, review information in the courtyard and give me mock tests.

As the months dragged on, I earned a B in every class. Maria was proud of me, but I still had many doubts about being in the classroom. I had questions about how my classmates would react to my being in a wheelchair. How would I get around the desks without running into them? How could I instruct a lesson and get to the whiteboard to illustrate the concept? Would I be able to hold the tempo of the class so they would not lose attention?

Not all classes were easy at CSUN, especially calculus, physics and linguistics. It would take me many hours to understand the concepts. Linguistics was tough because I had to understand grammar. Without a B average, I would be expelled from the program. I hated the thought of disappointing Maria. At night I poured out my heart to her and she consoled and encouraged me.

The last requirement was to pass the CBEST exit exam, a timed test covering reading, writing and arithmetic. One hundred prospective teachers sat in a large hall. We had one hour to finish the exam. Many of the students finished easily after 30 minutes. I had only finished three-fourths of the test by the end of the allotted hour. I turned the paper in and the waiting game began. I rolled to the mailbox every day until, weeks later, the official looking letter arrived from the Los Angeles Unified School District. Maria opened the document and I read this fateful word: "FAILED". I screamed as loud as I could, "N-o-o-o-o-o-o-o-o-o-o-o-o!!!" The neighbors came out one by one to see what terror was taking place in their sedate environment. I continued cursing and bemoaning my fate until one by one they retreated to their houses and peeked out from their curtains.

At Maria's urging I went back to the Disability Center to see what they could do. I did not want to go but I was running on empty. Maria was pregnant and I needed to support our family. I was told that because of my dyslexia the State would allow more time to take the test. Our friends' and Maria's prayers were answered. After three hours of testing I passed 60/61. I felt like I was in the clouds --like I could fly. I had jumped through the last hoop to become the first quadriplegic teacher in CSUN's 65-year history.

I still had questions about how to prepare lessons because my fingers were paralyzed. There was nobody in a scooter that I could talk to at college, but there were many inner voices saying, 'Just quit! You're nothing! You'll never amount to anything!' Nevertheless, in student teaching I proved that not only was I there for students educationally, but I was also there for them relationally. By example I showed them that they could overcome their difficulties. I let them chase me around the track during P.E. In the classroom every student had a job so they felt empowered. Students were managers for taking attendance, running notes to the office, managers to hold the telephone and even a manager for cockroaches and spiders.

One day the principal walked into my classroom and demanded to know where the teacher was. When I sheepishly called out from the corner, he looked at me doubtfully. I immediately shared my background, told him the students' names and started the first lesson in mathematics with an icebreaker. Rolling around the classroom, I wheeled behind inattentive students. I anticipated students' questions and made sure they comprehended what I was teaching.

At the end of the day the principal called me into his office. I sat silently while he reviewed his notes, my heart pounding. I was afraid he would say that my disability disqualified me from being a good teacher.

"Jack, I watched you today and you did a great job! My daughter is a gymnast and she knows what it takes to work hard, to discipline herself, to develop muscle strength—in short, to be a champion. I could see that you are applying what you learned in gymnastics to your work with these kids. I'd be happy to write a letter of recommendation to any principal stating that you will be a great teacher." I felt like a huge weight had just been lifted off my shoulders! I breathed a sigh of relief. I could be a provider for our family and an example of hope.

After student teaching, my first job was to teach fourth grade
at Broadous Elementary School in Pacoima, California. I was excited to
be an official educator in the Los Angeles Unified School District. The
school was located in a dangerous, gang-infested area. Gunshots rang
out during the night, terrorizing children who should have been fast
asleep. They saw shootings and stabbings. Their brothers were in gangs
and sometimes bullets would send a family member to the hospital. Students came to class with frightened demeanors and dark circles under
their eyes. Their parents, who more likely than not worked three jobs,
had dropped them off by 6:00 a.m. and would pick them up at six in the
evening.

I began teaching fourth grade in the middle of the fall semester. Two previous teachers had quit and several substitutes refused to
return. Nevertheless, I prayed for strength as I introduced myself and
told them my story. I felt like a new chapter of my life had begun. As I
wheeled around the room, a few 'cool' boys tried to thwart my attention
by throwing tacks under my scooter tires in hopes that they would de-
flate and I would be angry. What they failed to realize was that the tires
were foam-filled and could not be popped. However, those boys had
already forced two teachers to resign and intimidated several substitutes
into not returning. They did not give up easily. Plan B was to get me to
quit.

Still, I was shocked to think that they would do such a thing to
a person in a wheelchair! I could not teach a lesson with their talking,
smart attitudes and unwillingness to listen. By morning recess I felt so
disheartened that I had decided to quit. I turned my scooter around
and made a beeline for the principal's office. I did not look to the left or
to the right. I did not say 'Hi' to any teachers that first day. As I rolled
down the hallway at a fast clip, two veteran teachers saw me coming and
recognized the desperation of yet another first-day teacher. With wrists
interlocked, they blocked my path.

When I angrily told them that I was quitting, they said in unison, "Oh, no, you're not." They told me to turn my scooter around and
go back to my classroom where they would meet me after school. Reluctantly, I returned to my classroom. The next morning I had the students
immediately sit at their desks. Without smiling I divided the class into
two teams. I told them that each team would receive points for paying

attention. The team that had acquired the most points by Friday would receive a reward, a prize.

For the next two years these committed teachers taught me to control, praise and teach the class. They helped me plan lessons, set up bulletin boards and arrange the desks so that I could get around. They also showed me how to implement rules and consequences. In the evening I graded papers by dictating on my computer. Before school my teaching assistant would record grades, print out lessons plans and pick up supplies in the office.

When three students continued to be uncooperative, I tried to arrange parent conferences. Unfortunately, none of the parents were able to attend because of work schedules; therefore, the students had no accountability. They were occasionally sent to the principal's office or to another classroom so that they would be out of my frame of reference.

It took several years to realize that my students' lives were much different from mine. I had grown up with a caring mother who helped me with my homework after school. No gunshots rang out in the night. I had a full night's rest and respected my parents. Gangs had taught these kids not to listen to adults. But I learned to be consistent. I enforced the rules all year and it often took the whole year for some students to follow them.

I remember one particular student for whom I learned compassion. Andre had watched his father shoot his mother point-blank in the face, killing her. His father was sent to prison for life and Andre had to live with his aunt. Every day I'd find him under his desk, clutching the rails fearfully. I kept ordering him to come out from under the desk—"Now!" One month later in the middle of the night I heard a voice in my heart saying, "Love him."

The next day when I found Andre under the desk, I assured him compassionately that I cared for him and that he could stay under the desk as long as he wished. After that, Andre shared his feelings with the school psychologist each day. At the end of the school year he was able to sit at his desk. I think seeing me in a wheelchair helped him to realize that, even though I had suffered in a different way, I could relate to the harshness of life.

After my first year of teaching I chose to teach second grade the next year in hopes that younger kids would listen better. Not only had my first year of teaching been challenging, but also our first child, Christopher, had died in utero one week before his due date. Maria and I were in shock for many months. I questioned why God would allow us to experience such a deep loss.

On the first day of second grade the students were neatly dressed in new uniforms, backpacks and shoes. I confidently told parents that, yes, I was their child's teacher. I could read the doubts on their faces as they pondered whether to transfer their child to another class. The principal, Ms. Aareola, quietly stood behind me and reassured each one that Mr. Fischer was an excellent teacher.

The kids walked in and sat in their assigned seats. I introduced myself and told them I was looking forward to teaching them. As I wheeled around the classroom, I told them that I had not always been in a wheelchair. I had been a gymnast for thirteen years, second in the nation on the still rings. I showed them my picture. Hoping that younger kids would listen better, I went on to say that I was a world record holder for fingertip push-ups. I also told them at one time I was an acrobatic jazz dancer. I shared about my accident, that I had told my gym friends that I did not need any help to do a double backflip off the parallel bars. I asked them what could happen when they rode their bikes without holding onto the handlebars. Several students raised their hands. I called on one boy who said, "I'd fall on the ground!"

"You're right," I said. "When I decided not to ask for help, I swung through the bars too low and landed on my head. I broke my neck and I wasn't able to move." I went on to tell them that when you do not ask for help, you could get hurt.

"Any questions?" I asked them. One boy snickered, "How do you go to the bathroom?" Everyone laughed. I showed them my leg bag. Another student asked, "How do you take a shower?" I told him that I had a manual wheelchair and a roll-in shower that my wife helps me into.

Still another student raised his hand. "How do you drive?" When the recess bell rang, we all went out to my van and I showed them the remote control key that opened the side door. The ramp came down and they gasped. "It's like a spaceship, huh!" Next, I demonstrated how I transferred from the scooter to the driver's seat. I showed them the controls for the swivel seat and finally the hand control that allowed me to brake by pushing forward and to accelerate by pushing it down. I said the floor of the van had to be cut out and dropped one foot so that when I rolled into the van I would not hit my head. "Cool," some boys said. I knew I was making some friends that day and hopefully some attentive students.

I previewed each day's schedule and the subjects the class would be learning. They always asked, "When are we going to learn multiplication?" I promised that after they had memorized the twos, fives and tens, they could play multiplication bingo. Students who did well in my class were rewarded with stickers, candy, certificates, and teacher-helper jobs. I knew the boys, especially, would love to ride my scooter. I told them and the girls that the last day of school each one would get to ride it while I sat in a chair. I knew they looked forward to that. Every week or so I would remind them that doing their work, coming to school on time, and raising their hands would give them a chance to ride my scooter. Their faces would light up.

Teaching 2nd Grade

Some of the boys and girls were recent immigrants from Mexico and did not know English very well. I let them know that I had been a second-grader once and had not made good grades. In fact, I had done so poorly that I had flunked second-grade, but now I actually was teaching second grade! They were encouraged after hearing that. I told them that if they dreamed big and tried their best, they could accomplish anything. My young students began to relax and feel more confident about earning good grades and having fun in second grade.

Our class had many managers. Some put a dropped marker back into my hand. A paper manager passed out papers, collected homework and ran notes and memos to and from the office. Other managers would choose a student to put their answer on the bulletin board, take down old work and file it in the homework boxes. A closet manager organized backpacks. I even employed a 'pee' manager for nervous students who occasionally wet their pants. Almost nobody volunteered for that job except for one unruly boy that would do anything for badly wanted attention. In addition, I had a cockroach manager! I chose a boy seeking inappropriate attention. He was always happy to step on them and toss them out the door. A telephone manager would take the phone off the hook and hold it up to my ear. Often after school, managers filed papers, erased whiteboards and swept floors.

At lunch time I had a student manager place my lunch next to the computer from right to left starting with carrots, then a breakfast bar, sandwich and finally a treat—a piece of chocolate, which I would give to my helper as a reward. Eating has always been a challenge as a quadriplegic. But I'm thankful that with many foods I am able to use my limited dexterity to feed myself. For instance, with a sandwich I would ask for the bread and meat to be placed near the edge of the desk or table. I would then place my clamped fingers below the edge of the surface and pull up, which had the effect of opening my fingers. Then I would dig the unclenched fingers into the top of the bread and pull toward me. 70% of the time this worked just fine and 30% of the time I went hungry, but 100% of the time I did it my way.

After I finished my lunch, I'd often hear a knock on the door. Girls frequently gave up their playtime on the field to come help me set up for the afternoon science or history lesson. It made them feel good, plus they liked the idea of knowing what the lesson was going to be before everyone else. Our class was like a colony of ants working toward a common goal—becoming lifelong learners.

A math 'student teacher' would demonstrate each step of her problem on the overhead projector. If the answer was correct, her name would be added to a list on the board. Right answers earned five checks. On Fridays each five checks earned a candy. They could earn a limitless number of candies.

I told the class that there were many ways to solve a problem in whatever subject we were studying. A student who could show me another way would also get five checks. Our class ran like a well–oiled machine! I also encouraged English language learners to do what they could do to show one or more steps to an answer. I wanted them to feel empowered, to know that I would not just call on the "smart" students.

I reminded them that I had one time failed second-grade because I could not understand how to give answers in reading, writing and arithmetic. That sense of failure had gone with me throughout my life. My job as a teacher was to stop the negative voices telling them the lie that they were stupid and could not learn. I showed my class how to draw and paint Van Gogh's *Starry Night*. "But teacher, I can't draw." With an encouraging smile, I would say, "Yes, you can. Watch what I do..."

Writing stories was difficult for most kids. In an approach called *the writing process*, students were asked to brainstorm a particular subject. I recounted the story of my eye accident and then had them write about a time they got hurt. They were told to 'free write' as many details as they could without lifting their pencil. Then came the hard work, editing to make sure their words made sense and were on the topic. If they were writing about a birthday party and skipped to a vacation, I would tell them to go back to the original thought. I encouraged them to use creative words that added flavor to their stories.

Rewriting the story could be very boring and tedious. To make that part of the process easier, I had them pair up with a friend at their tables. They listened to each other's stories and wrote down comments and suggestions. After the story was rewritten, they made sure they had complete sentences and correct punctuation.

This process was helpful to English language learners who also read children's books as models of good writing. I encouraged them to use colors to illustrate their stories. I let my students know that the concepts that they were learning applied to life. For example, an engineer takes steps to design a bridge. *The writing process* could also come in handy working on a storyboard for a new movie. The budding authors pinned their final copies on the writers' bulletin board under their names. During the school's open house, oftentimes a child would grab his parent's hand and proudly pull him or her over to the writing bulletin board.

Studying the life cycle of a frog gave students information about how life begins and transforms. When the class studied the ocean and sea life, I shared some of my scuba diving experiences. Sometimes the science lesson would be to make cold slime that bounced like a rubber ball. As a prize, students could take some home. But my passion was to show God's creative hand in nature--the color and design of flowers, butterflies and saltwater fish, 'wowing' the senses. Having my students slow down and observe life cycles opened up their world. At the end of each year, our class took a field trip to the California Science Center.

The students always looked forward to holidays like Valentine's Day. We played educational games, plus Maria would make cupcakes decorated with red and white sprinkles. At Christmas she would surprise the boys and girls with gifts.

Sometimes if I had a urinary tract infection my body would freeze. The bell would ring and I could not move. The kids would know after a few minutes that something was wrong if I had not lined up with them. I would often hear them run up the ramp to ask if I was all right. I would calmly tell them that I was not. My teacher's assistant would have to force my legs back onto the floorboard of my scooter. Shaking and with a sweaty head, I would tell the students that I had to leave to see my doctor. My assistant's challenge was to open the van, pry my stiff legs into the driver's seat and then call the doctor to let him know I needed my catheter changed. In pain and confusion, I would drive the freeway to the doctor's office. My stubborn will and gymnastics background helped me to exert mind over matter.

Some days I wanted to quit. Holding the large teacher's book in my lap while rolling the scooter into the classroom was a trial. I was frustrated by the constant fallen markers, the telephone ringing, test papers falling, not being able to turn on the overhead projector and having to back my scooter into place next to the overhead so I could point to a math problem. Sometimes I needed a break and I let my TA teach for ten minutes while I leaned my chair back.

My second year I was so angry with a student who would not listen that I told him I was going to put duct tape on his mouth. He did not believe me, but I did tape his mouth shut with the help of my assistant. I also told him that if he got out of his chair he would have to sit on the floor. I had my assistant put masking tape around his chair so that he could not leave the circle until break time. When the principal and parents found out what I had done, I was told that if I ever did that again I would be fired. Another year I was really angry because my class was so rowdy and disrespectful that I rammed my scooter into a desk, flipping it and its occupant backwards onto the floor. The class was quiet after that!

Getting to school was difficult most days. My legs were cramped and my body stiffened up. On rainy days, holding an umbrella and making my way to the front door of my classroom was a challenge. The umbrella was not nearly as easy for me as The Sandwich Trick and I often relied upon the kindness of colleagues and students to help me remain dry. The muddy wheels tracked dirt all over the floor.

Occasionally my leg bag would open up. I tried not to let the students know what had happened. Some students thought it was the person next to them that had urinated on the tile. I'd have to call the office to get a sub. I was humbled many times by losing control of my bowels. I would tell the office that I had to go home and a teaching coach would fill in for me. When I would call Maria, she was very kind and compassionate saying, "Oh, I'm so sorry this is happening to you."

I'd drive home in tears, questioning why God was allowing this. Did He have no compassion? How much suffering could I take? Crying in confusion, I would pull into our driveway where Maria would meet me and put her arm around my shoulder. She would take me down to the bathroom, clean me up and listen to my woes. Each time that happened our relationship grew stronger.

Finally, I was able to let go of questioning God. I had a family to feed and a job to do. My gymnastics background and my parents' modeling had taught me perseverance. Tomorrow would be a new day and I was prepared to give it all I could, no matter what the circumstances. The harder the challenge, the better!

Sometimes my scooter would break down and I had to have the students push me off the playground and down to the office where I would call Harold at Ability Advance to let him know I needed to have then fix it. They were very kind in fixing it right away because they knew I needed it for school.

Every once in a while my principal would leave a note of encouragement, but few teachers ever said anything to me about how hard I tried. I don't know whether they were consumed with their own workload or whether they were afraid of embarrassing me. A colleague telling me that I was doing a good job carried me over for many weeks. The teachers accepted me as one of their own. They made my life easier by opening doors and making copies of homework packets.

During annual teacher reviews, a group of administrators and principals from around the San Fernando Valley would observe me. On their clipboards they recorded what I was teaching, whether current student work was on display and whether I could maintain class control. They stayed for ten minutes watching every move I made and seeing if the students were paying attention. They never said anything to me, but their faces reflected a sense of wonder that I was doing such a good job. One administrator confided, "I don't know how you do it--maintain the class with high test scores. I can tell you there are far worse teachers out there and they're on their feet."

The last day of the school year I let each of my students ride my scooter in a racetrack maze on the playground. Students from other classes wanted to be in my room the next year just for that reason. It was always emotional watching the kids leave, saying their goodbyes until next year when they would be in third grade. Most of them would come back in the fall to say, "Hi" for the first few weeks of the new year. Many students would visit me years later, all grown up and well dressed. They would say in an upbeat tone, "Hey, Mr. Fischer, how are you?"

I'd step back into my memory bank saying, "Is that you, Ronaldo?"

"Yep! All grown up, I'm doin' fine."

Other former students would tell me proudly that they had graduated from high school and were in college. I could tell I had influenced them in conquering the odds. Seeing them made me feel proud to be a teacher because, until then, I had never really known whether or not I was making a difference.

In the winter of 2012, I was forced to retire early due to urinary tract infections, weight loss and muscle weakness. I could no longer drive or speak clearly. It was a sad day and my heart broke, knowing I would never teach again. I received a commendation for being a role model from the California State House of Representatives. My colleagues acknowledged me on retirement day with a one-minute standing ovation. Many came up to me in tears saying they would miss me. I was in tears as well at having to give up what I had loved doing for twenty years.

Together, my students and I had learned valuable life lessons: to persevere through trials, to be thankful for what we have and to bring hope to someone who is hurting.

My grace is sufficient for you, for my strength is made perfect in weakness.

(2 Corinthians 12:9)

Life is hard. I thought when I accepted Christ that the road ahead would be smooth. On the contrary, the road has been difficult. With aging, the path has become even more so. I have moments when I feel hopeless and wallow in self-pity. Initiating a meaningful, adult conversation is a hassle. Being seated in my wheelchair means that I usually have to look up like a child when I am talking to people. Well-meaning mothers discourage their children from looking at me. They shush questions about why I might be in a wheelchair. If they only knew that I would welcome a lively conversation about my experience!

Living with attendants and depending on machines makes for a lonely life. Outside the home, where my precious Maria and Abigail give me all the loving care a husband or father could ever ask for, I can't really expect others to understand the long distance runner's mentality of solitude I experience day to day. All this is compounded by having to see my urologist weekly and being on a strict sugar-free and dairy-free diet. Slipping up and enjoying an ice cream cone causes a severe bladder infection. The floracortizone I take every morning to raise my blood pressure takes two hours to work. In the interim I fall in and out of consciousness in front of the bathroom mirror. If I forget to take my meds when I am out, my joints tighten painfully.

In recent years I was diagnosed with Parkinson's disease. This weakens the muscles gradually until they are no longer of much use and barely controllable. When I learned I had this to add to my heaping pile of afflictions, my mind ran the gamut of emotions from doubt to anger, fear, and finally acceptance. Recently I saw David Letterman's interview with Michael J. Fox and cried out, "I'm fifty-nine, Lord. Am I going to be even more humiliated? Haven't I suffered enough?"

I constantly struggle with trusting God because He has not healed me the way I hoped. Once I attended a spiritual warfare conference. The speaker emphatically claimed that the Bible said I would be healed if I had enough faith. I believed him and received prayer for healing. Nothing changed. Nothing! Dejected, I rolled my scooter down a dark hallway and yelled, "God if you're there, why don't you heal me? I've prayed 5,000 times and you don't answer. Jesus healed everyone who asked. Why not me? I am suffering. I hate You! I don't want to live like this anymore. Just kill me!"

It was then that I envisioned a terrifying spiritual entity that was attempting to attack me. Realizing that we do not fight against flesh and blood but against powerful, spiritual forces changed my worldview. I heard God's voice say that, although He could end my life if He wanted to, it was not my time. I vowed that evening not to take my own life. Although I was not healed, I yielded to God's will. I turned my scooter around and rolled back to the van where Maria was waiting.

Some years later I experienced the miraculous! In the summer of 2001 I noticed that after people at church prayed for me, my right leg began to move. One afternoon in the backyard as I was standing in my chair, I lifted my right foot off the grass and moved it forward two inches. I could not believe it! My faith level rose astronomically. I told Maria. The next day I looked online for parallel bars and found a pair on Craigslist for $600. They arrived in a U-Haul truck.

That evening I stood for the first time in over ten years. Looking down on my scooter was a strange experience. I felt blood rush through my legs and pulse in my toes. After a few days I could lift my right leg. After three weeks I took my first step. I watched my feet walk as though they belonged to someone else. After a month I could walk to the end of the bars and back. I felt on top of the world! After three months I was able to walk back and forth three times. I walked like this for five years. I would occasionally fall and, afraid that I would seriously injure myself, Maria begged me to stop. Because our relationship outweighed my sense of freedom, the parallel bars went back onto Craigslist.

In spite of this wonderful experience, I still sometimes feel abandoned by God. Praying can be difficult. As I circle the fruit-tree checkpoints in my backyard, I use my smartphone to read the Bible and worship. When I feel grief over my terrible loss, I consider what God has graciously given me—my supportive wife and daughter, my loving family, my dog Ollie. I am grateful not for only these enriching relationships but also for the conveniences of an accessible van, technology and my comfortable home. I have enjoyed a long, fulfilling career and been able to re-experience underwater beauty, to travel and to make a positive contribution to the disabled community and my church. In spite of my disability—and perhaps in some ways because of it—I live a full and rich life. Negative thoughts dissipate as I praise God!

Afterword

If God's first two children, Adam and Eve, could go back and have a do-over . . . they undoubtedly would. Don't you think?

I ask my friend Jack Fischer a similar question.

"If you could change your life, if you could go back and miss practice that day or swallow your pride and accept a spotter to help you, would you do it?"

Jack tells me there was a time he wouldn't have hesitated answering, "Yes. What do you think?"

Upon further reflection, though, he gives a different, more thoughtful response to the alternate path question.

"I know now I wouldn't take back anything," he says quietly. "If I had completed my exercise, gotten up off the mat, taken a shower and changed into street clothes on October 23, 1979, I would have missed the great depth that has accompanied all the suffering as a result of my injury. I think of the people I would never have met and the challenges I've overcome that have made me a better man."

To hear him tell it, the pre-injury Jack was, at times, a bit of an ass.

"If the accident never happened I would be a completely different person today. I was a self-centered guy who rarely thought about more than one day at a time. To be honest, I was a real jerk!"

"Going through this final indignity of Parkinson's," he tells me, "has changed the way I think and react when I meet someone who is unable to communicate. I have empathy for the slow, slurred speech."

This compassion empowers Jack to share with those he encounters what he's learned about God's unceasing love. It frees him to engage anyone in conversation without fear or shame. I've seen Jack bring any topic around to The Father's Love. It's a thing of beauty to watch.

"How can I not tell them how I see the finish line and the more that I suffer the more appealing God's eternal promise looks? In that moment I've been granted a slice of moral authority in their eyes to speak of a tomorrow with no pain, no suffering--only glory. I know I have a bit more credibility now than when I was 30 and wallowing in self-pity.

"I share how I dream of the day when the race is run, my chest breaks the runner's tape and my exultant arms raise quite naturally over a head that is basking in glory.

"These days I am experiencing a transition where the line between Earth and Heaven is becoming more blurred. I think anyone with multiple physical disabilities looks forward, eventually, to the finish line.

"I do not treasure my disabilities. But they are a way for me to refocus my eyes from looking down at my navel to gazing up at my Lord.

"None of us welcome pain or hard times or falling behind in the race. We don't like being chosen last on the playing field or being unable to comprehend what we are learning as others seem to be able to do. We want to excel at these things and prefer not being shoved in the corner by playground bullies. We may feel at times that we are being left out while comparing ourselves to the 'best and brightest.' "

For Jack, I believe it all boils down to being content.

"Through my broken neck God allowed one arrogant gymnast to learn the Proverbs 14 lesson that pride comes before the fall. Like the latest new car commercials, the world teaches us to be fast, sleek, smooth and seductive as we hug those curves in the road.

"Christians prefer not to be seen when we don't look so good. Yet it's in these times when we are weak that God is strong."

Jack is grateful for the time remaining with the people he loves and admires. There is much to occupy his time, mind and heart in the interim between here and the finish line. He paints, sketches and has written several unpublished books he hopes to bring to fruition.

When I see Jack out on the patio with sketchpad at the ready he is at the edge of the family garden. In that moment where greens and reds blend with the colors and textures of remembrance—at that place where Jack gazes into the garden . . . for a moment I think of Adam and Eve in their own lush garden.

Like Jack, they lived a seemingly perfect existence, protected from tomorrow by the comfort of today. Like Jack, they committed a prideful act, ensuring a never-before-known vulnerability to the world.

And like my dear friend with his premature trip to the gym mat, their abrupt departure from Eden was the beginning of an adventure they wouldn't have asked for. But didn't they each grow to understand the price of their sin along with the Father's grace in what came later? Didn't they make peace with their own flawed natures rather than wallow in the thicket or waste away in a hospital bed?

To see this man attempting, from the perch of a powerful electric wheelchair, to capture on paper a slice of fragile beauty is a joy to watch. It's here, in this moment, I get a powerful sense of The Struggle Of Today versus the Promise of Tomorrow. It is the ever-present clash of the earthly and eternal that will never find resolution on this side of the divide.

Here in Jack and Maria's small garden you might not see the connection. You might miss the similarities. You wouldn't think there was that much in common between Jack Fischer and the original sinners.

For the first part of his life there seemed no common bond at all. But here in the garden, set away from the pressures and realities of life, the connection comes to me like an old Polaroid snapshot, blending its muddy coloring slowly into focus.

Jack. Adam. Eve. Their lives were forever altered; never again the same. But preservation and salvation manifested in the form of Grace and Provision from The Father.

And it all began . . . after the fall.

– Michael O'Connor

July 2017

Acknowledgements

My dear Abigail, words are inadequate to describe the pride Mom and I have in how you consistently seize life's opportunities and challenges while living life adventurously with heart and tenacity. I greatly admire and love you, my daughter.

Thank you, Dad, for the years of commitment, being there through the eye and neck accidents. You and Mom provided enduring support and unwavering love through my darkest days. I hope the words on these pages reflect the love you both gave to me. Thank you Dad for your example of character, generosity, discipline, and perseverance.

Joni Eareckson Tada, thank you for being my mentor through the past 35 years. Your dedication and love for Jesus Christ has inspired me to comfort people who need encouragement, as I've been able.

Thank you, Jeanne Fischer Bolt, for your support and tears while praying for me, sending cards and phoning with heartfelt concern. We have shared many wonderful moments through the years and I look forward to many more.

Thank you, Pastor Ken Bolt, for your prayers and words of wisdom through the Scriptures. You have been there for me through the difficult years and I pray your ministry will continue to be blessed.

Thank you, Doug Fischer, my brother through birth and through Christ. I pray for you as a fellow brother who suffers in a totally different way, yet has a good attitude and loving heart. I can't wait to see you again!

Pastor Bill Dwyer, thank you for your leadership and love for our family. Thank you for praying for God's will to be done in our lives. You have been faithful in preaching the Word, and I pray God's blessings on your family.

Thank you Lynn and Jo Cory for the many years of deep friendship. Your love and caring has always been more personal than professional to us. Thank you for knowing the difference and acting upon it.

Thank you Rosie Clandos for researching scientific terms to make the rehab chapters more interesting. Your smile, good words and confidence encourages me always,

Thank you, Kevin Grable, for the many Saturdays at Mimi's Café writing down notes for the book. You are a dear brother, tireless in your efforts to help!

Thank you, Michael O'Connor, for shepherding this book through the publishing process. I'll never forget the time you and Kevin Grable drove me to the Mount Hermon Christian Writer's Conference. We had a lot of fun and wonderful memories!

Thank you, Sally O'Connor, for believing in me. Your example in song, writing and as a dedicated mother and wife demonstrates Christ's love in a strong way.

Dr. Rene Osman, Dr. Robert Klein, Dr. Mehran Okhovat, and Dr. Joel Rosen: each of you have extended not only medical expertise, but true care for my well-being which has gone above and beyond. Blessings to you all.

Thank you Peter and Candy Yost for housing me after college, leading the Athletes in Action team and your many prayers for my recovery.

Thank you, Paul Tickenoff. You were there as I lay still on the mat with a broken neck and I will always be grateful it was you. You exhibited leadership for Dad and me in the darkest moments. You will always be in my heart and I know we'll be able to do cartwheels together again in heaven!

Thank you, Bee Thoma, for becoming my friend during those early days at Athletes in Action and maintaining close friendship through the years.

Thank you, Steve Shepherd, for the many wonderful times we had at the gym and in backyards during the endless summers of our long, lost youth!

Thank you, John Golbeck, for four years of rooming together at Indiana State University. Each day brought smiles and laughter from our clowning around that are still with me after all this time.

Thank you Hinsdale Central High School coaches Tony Canino, Paul Omi, Harrison Bull and Neil Krupika for your expertise and commitment to molding champions for life.

Thank you ISU gymnastics coach Roger Council for believing in me and for the many hours you committed your expertise to making us national champions in 1977.

Thank you gym buddies: Barry Woodward, Chris Dolson, Bob Mellon and Kurt Thomas for the wonderful memories at I.S.U.

Thank you, Kean Chua, for transcribing my stories from spoken word to 12 point Helvetica. I couldn't have done this without you. Thank you for taking care of my needs in such a detailed manner. You're a close friend.

Thank you Lynn Miller, facilitator for W.A.G.S. (Wilkenson Author's Group for Seniors) for your encouragement and ongoing editing advice for my writings. Your leadership in our group is a real gift that keeps all of us writing great stories!

Marlene Williams, thank you for the many letters and prayers that encouraged me to keep on sharing God's Word! I look forward to spending many more moments with you and Wendy in heaven!

Thank you, Tim Micklin, for your support and prayers those first years of my disability. Your smile and laughter lightened my worries. Thank you for transforming your house into a handicap-accessible home just for me. God's richest blessings on your ministries.

Thank you Harold and Darrell at Ability Advance in Mission Hills, CA, for repairing my scooter on such short notice so I could teach.

Thank you fellow teachers at Broadous Elementary School who were always available with help even before my needs had become apparent. When my stress levels were on overload, you were there to help relieve the pressure. I will always be grateful for your loving care.

Thank you, Jane Willard, for your encouragement and friendship these last two years. You are a treasure to the Body of Christ.

Thank you Fred Massey, Claire O'Brien, Gail O'Brien, and Gwen O'Brien for your support and prayers through the years. Thank you Anne O'Brien for giving me such a beautiful daughter and companion!

Thank you Mark and Gale Landstrom, Bill Kolb, Scott Dusing, Joe Ellis, Paul and Martha Bellamy for the wonderful years of friendship. Your support has made all the difference.

Thank you to my caregiver, Wilson Hernandez. Your concern to make me feel important and treat me as a friend has made me look forward to seeing you and developing a personal friendship with your family as well.

Thank you Judy Spore for your genuine love and skill as my art coach. Isn't it a joy that while you teach me to paint we can both share in Christ's love together!

Thank you Maricela Parra for your professional care while keeping me healthy. I look forward to our weekly chats and conversations.

Thank you Orrin Turbow for your expert handling of our legal matters through the years and the friendship we enjoy.

Thank you Josh Rubinstein and Shari Rubinstein at Restoration Press for your expert design and final edit skills and for joining in this vision ministering to those in need of hope.

Finally, a very special thanks:

Thank you Joyce Lister who performed the most remarkable job of editing a manuscript any writer could hope for. I know the hours upon hours you spent making sense of my mass of ideas, disorganized as they started, was a gift you gave to the Lord as much as it was for me. I will forever be in your debt, my friend.

About The Authors

Jack Fischer was a world-class gymnast and world record holder until an accident cut his career short in 1979, leaving him paralyzed from the neck down. In 1992 he became the first quadriplegic teacher in the history of the Los Angeles Unified School District and taught for twenty years. Jack lives in Southern California with his wife Maria. They have a daughter, Abigail. He welcomes your comments at: jackandmariafischer@gmail.com .

Joyce Lister holds B.A. and M.A. degrees in English and has taught writing for over three decades. She and her husband are active in the Valley Vineyard Christian Fellowship (Reseda, CA) and have been friends with Jack and Maria Fischer for more than thirty years. She resides in Camarillo, CA with her husband Dave and her tuxedo cat, Teddy.